The Year of the Bear

The story of Warwickshire's 2004 Championship triumph

by Brian Halford

With a Foreword by John Inverarity
and an Introduction from Nick Knight

The Parrs Wood Press
Manchester

THE PARRS WOOD PRESS
St Wilfrid's Enterprise Centre
Royce Road, Manchester, M15 5BJ
www.parrswoodpress.com

ISBN: 1 903158 64 8

Printed in Malta by Gutenberg Press

To Cubby

Acknowledgements

Thanks to Mary Bonner, Nick Archer, Mike Beddow, the *Birmingham Post* and *Mail*, the *Brighton Evening Argus*, Phil Britt, Robert Brooke, Keith Cook, Simon Hollyhead, John Inverarity, Nick Knight, Steve Murphy, Phil O'Farrell, Joan Rutledge, Andy Searle, Colin Summerton, Bruce Talbot and David Wainwright.

Contents

FOREWORD

by John Inverarity

In the lead up to the 2004 season our expectations were modest. Our preparation was thorough, and our determination to do our very best at all times was both high and well-defined.

At season's end we were very excited about our success, and a little stunned that it had come our way. Winning the championship is not something that happens often. A strong and established club such as Warwickshire had won it on only five previous occasions in 110 years - in 1911, 1951, 1972, 1994 and 1995.

And now 2004. Winning the championship is a relatively rare and precious event. Let us all savour the achievement while always, of course, being aware of the need to move on for the challenges of 2005 and the years beyond.

How did we win? The first thing that comes to mind is that we batted very strongly and very consistently. We had batting strength throughout our line-up. The top five collectively had a very good season. And when they failed as a unit others in the middle order (Dougie Brown, Brad Hogg and Tony Frost) or the lower order came to the rescue, and ensured that we posted a good first-innings score.

The following are remarkable statistics. The two lowest totals we were bowled out for in 2004 were 295 (against Northamptonshire after we had secured the title) and 317. Of our 16 first-innings totals we exceeded 400 on 11 occasions, and we were never bowled out in the second innings. In doing this the individual players, and the team as a whole, persistently displayed tremendous resilience, character and a never-say-die attitude.

Highlights? Too many to mention here, but I wish to refer to the example of four players.

Ian Bell scored 1,498 championship runs from 25 innings, including a double-century, five centuries and four half-centuries. He "did the business". For a cricket team to play well and gain momentum - and win matches - then individual players need to perform. They need to shape a game or alter its course. This is what Ian Bell did.

Nick Knight batted well, but it was his captaincy that was a particularly telling factor. He gave his body, his soul, his all to this role and he gave it in an unassumingly firm and kindly way. He commanded great respect and loyalty.

Dougie Brown also made an extraordinary contribution. When others lapsed, he stood tall. He made hugely valuable runs and he was our highest wicket-taker with 38. In the final match at Northampton he scored a century and took five wickets in an innings, a feat seldom achieved. But it was also Dougie's constant generosity of spirit to all in the team, his patience, courtesy, belief and optimism that contributed strongly to the momentum that carried us through.

For Michael Powell, 2003 was a difficult season. The character and example he displayed throughout 2004 was, together with his excellent performances with the bat, a central component in our victorious campaign. His first appearance in the team was on May 25th when we were at home to Worcestershire, and his 49, batting at number six, was most significant in turning the game. He next played against Kent at Beckenham on June 23rd, opened the batting in place of the injured Nick Knight, and scored 134. Character, determination and "doing the business" abounded.

There are many others who contributed much and many other examples I could cite, but this is only a foreword. I will conclude by stating that I feel privileged to have been

Foreword by John Inverarity

associated with such a pleasant, dedicated, deserving and responsive group of cricketers. I also enjoyed my many chats with the author of this book during the season as he chronicled our progress around the country for readers of the *Birmingham Evening Mail*. He is ideally placed to capture the spirit of a memorable season in the pages that follow.

INTRODUCTION

by Nick Knight

As we prepared for last season John Inverarity and I agreed we wanted to get an extra five per cent out of each player.

In most cases we succeeded. In a few we probably got more than five per cent. In one or two maybe not that much, which is something to work on next season, but individually and collectively they upped their game and ended up as deserved winners of the championship - a feat of which Warwickshire County Cricket Club can be very proud.

The county season is a long one, and the players should take enormous credit for the mental strength they showed to hold their nerve all the way through. Remaining unbeaten is quite a feat in itself. But the seeds of success were sown long before even the first match in April. The previous autumn, Simon Hollyhead and Gerhard Mostert were working with the players towards sending them into the 2004 season fitter than they had ever been before. That was a major factor in our success.

In our first two games, against Middlesex and Gloucestershire, our cricket disappointed me. But then we went down to Cambridge University and played Shropshire in the C&G Trophy, and although those might not seem the most important games in fact they were very significant. We took them seriously and tried to win them as early as possible, and that gave us momentum.

There were many fine performances to follow but I would pick out the victory over Surrey at Guildford as a crucial game. We had just come through a rough three weeks in one-day cricket, where we didn't play that well in the Twenty20 and lost a C&G Trophy semi-final we should have won. But at Guildford we played some terrific cricket and beat a very good side convincingly. That proved to me the mental strength of the team. After the defeat to Worcestershire in the C&G Trophy I was asked what I would have to do to lift the team again, and I said "nothing". So it proved. They are a superbly motivated set of players. Throughout the season they played with a lot of pride in their own performance, and also pride in representing Warwickshire. Taking the Bears back to the top of the tree meant an awful lot to us. Now we've got to keep going.

Winning the championship is not something that happens to a county too often. The achievement of Warwickshire's players in 2004 will go down in history with our predecessors of 1911, 1951, 1972, 1994 and 1995, and that is illustrious company indeed. It is a feat that will live on in history, and I am pleased that Brian Halford has come up with a detailed and colourful account, which will enable cricket-lovers of the present and the future to read in detail about how the title was won.

THE CAST

APRIL 2004

NEIL ABBERLEY.
Batting coach. Played 258 matches for Warwickshire, scoring more than 10,000 runs between 1964 and 1979. Also took five wickets including a best of two for 19 at the Parks in 1972, when his seven canny overs narrowly failed to prevent Oxford University clinching a thrilling two-wicket win with two balls to spare.

IAN BELL.
First turned up at Edgbaston nets aged 12, pinged the bowlers around for fun and has been labelled a future England star ever since. Fresh from a winter's work on his batting and mental approach in Perth, he should be ready to put a couple of uneven seasons behind him and make serious advances.

DOUGIE BROWN.
All-rounder who made his debut in the 1994 championship season and soon embedded himself deep in the Bears' team and affections. A fighter but more than a fighter, he is one of the most productive all-rounders in Warwickshire's history.

NEIL CARTER.
Left-arm seamer and aggressive batsman. Exciting pinch-hitter and bowler who often seems to miss rather than find the edge. Harvested the unluckiest analysis in the history of cricket in the championship match against Lancashire at Old Trafford in 2002.

13

The Year of the Bear

TONY FROST.
Joined the Bears in 1997 and has since contested the wicket-keeper's role with Keith Piper. Less naturally gifted with the gloves than Piper but a more focused and productive batsman, with a first-class average of 24.59 compared to Piper's 19.99.

ASHLEY GILES.
A virtual stranger to the Edgbaston dressing room in recent years, having been England's property ever since central contracts came in. Still to win over a section of Warwickshire supporters, just like cricket followers countrywide, but can point to more than 4,000 runs and 400 wickets in first-class cricket.

BRAD HOGG.
Australian all-rounder. An intriguing overseas signing. Aggressive batsman and livewire fielder, but the 33-year-old's left-arm wrist-spin - he arrives with a first-class bowling average of 40 - is an unknown quantity.

SIMON HOLLYHEAD.
Fitness and conditioning coach at Edgbaston since 2000. Birmingham-born, avid West Bromwich Albion supporter and highly rated architect of the Bears' fitness and medical back-up regime. Likes beetroot.

JOHN INVERARITY.
Starting the second half of his two-year contract as coach and eager to build upon a middling first year. Vastly experienced - he captained Western Australia with great success and played six Tests for Australia - and highly respected by the players. One of few men to have scored a first-class century in Stoke-on-Trent.

The Cast - April 2004

NICK KNIGHT.
Retired from international one-day-cricket after his 100th appearance for England in 2003, but has batted better than ever in the last two seasons for Warwickshire. Replaces Michael Powell as captain, eager to avoid the batting slump which plagued his predecessor during three years in the job.

GERHARD MOSTERT.
Physio born and bred in Kroonstad, Free State, South Africa. Joined Warwickshire in 2001 and has become a pivotal member of the back-room team.

STEVE PERRYMAN.
Bowling coach. Big-hearted seam bowler for the Bears between 1974 and 1981 before ending his career with a brief spell at Worcestershire. Brummie through and through, passionate Birmingham City fan and coffee-lover. Not a total stranger to the pages of the *Racing Post*.

MICHAEL POWELL.
Stepped down as captain in September 2003 after three years of wading through club politics seriously eroded his batting average. Faces a battle to force his way into the 1st XI but, a real fighter, will relish the challenge.

DEWALD PRETORIUS.
Fast-bowler who has played four Tests for South Africa but sees his future in England. Has signed a three-year deal at Edgbaston. Will play in the first XI in early and late season before and after Heath Streak's input.

ALAN RICHARDSON.
Wholehearted and underrated seamer from Staffordshire. Fresh from a winter in Australia, monitoring from afar the

fortunes of his beloved Stoke City, and expected to fulfil the main stock-bowling role in a thin-looking pace attack.

HEATH STREAK.
Zimbabwe captain originally scheduled to arrive in June when his country's Test commitments would allow, and leave in early September to lead them in the ICC Champions Trophy. With Zimbabwean cricket in turmoil, now available straight away but will stick to his original arrival date and then stay all season.

NAQAASH TAHIR.
Twenty-year-old seam-bowler of rich promise and a useful lower-order batsman. Troubled by injuries last season but left his imprint on Michael Powell's big toe with a pre-season yorker that ruled the captain out for six weeks.

JONATHAN TROTT.
South Africa-born but fuelled by desire to play for England. Announced himself to Warwickshire in 2002 with a double century on debut for the 2nd XI. On his 1st XI bow the following year he lodged a ton against Sussex and went on to amass 763 runs at 42.38. Big future.

JIM TROUGHTON.
Established himself in the Bears' 1st XI in 2002 with a string of centuries and continued that form early in 2003 to earn a call-up for England's one-day squad. Had a thin time there though, and found runs hard to come by when he returned to Edgbaston.

MARK WAGH.
Former Oxford University captain. A stylish batsman and improving off-spin bowler. Long-regarded as a potential England player, at 27 should be ready to take the next step if it is to come.

DAVID WAINWRIGHT.
Scorer. The most consistent run-gatherer on the staff. Highly respected by the players, for whom he is an invaluable source of information.

One

v Middlesex
at Edgbaston

Friday, April 16th:

Middlesex 115 for 3

The big day. The opening day of the season. For seven months everything has been geared to this. Ever since the valedictory clack of bat on ball last September preparations, devised and supervised by fitness and conditioning coach Simon Hollyhead and physio Gerhard Mostert, have been building up to today.

The players were given time off in late September and October. From the first week of November they attended various David Lloyd Fitness Centres two or three times a week for a rigorous programme of "prehabilitation" (recovering from injuries before they happen - geddit?). This stepped up to three times per week in the New Year as the players undertook intense strength and conditioning work which included cycling, rowing, swimming and many laps round the Alexander Stadium.

Not so long ago county cricketers' pre-season preparations were largely fag-and-pint fuelled with an occasional net slipped in. The current lot had electrical impulses sent round their bodies to measure body-fat percentages from which specific exercise programmes were calculated for each individual. Hydration levels were meticulously checked and rechecked. In March it stepped up to full-time work with more cricket-specific drills. Bowlers delivered longer spells. Batters pored over videos of their technique. Fielders flung themselves around the Edgbaston outfield.

Sir Steve Redgrave visited Edgbaston to talk about winning. There was a two-day bonding session in Shrewsbury. Several 7am cross-country runs honed bodies further towards the required state of perfection so that on April 16, this day, the first of the long, arduous season, those bodies would be poised, ready for action. Here they are; the players like coiled springs, athletes at the peak of their physical powers. And for most of the day they sat on their arses in the dressing-room watching it rain.

It's fair to say the 2004 season sneaked rather than burst into existence. Only 37.3 overs were possible and in those the cricket was largely so tortuous that the 66.3 overs lost to rain were more entertaining.

The "action" began after an hour's delay at noon when Warwickshire won the toss and put Middlesex in. Sven Koenig faced the first ball of a pristine, freshly-unwrapped season from Dewald Pretorius and joined an illustrious list of batsmen including Fred Gardner (from Trevor Bailey in 1950), Geoff Boycott (from Bob Willis in 1981) and Michael Powell (from Alan Mullally in 2001) who failed to smite the first ball of an Edgbaston summer straight back over the bowler's head for six.

Instead Koenig defended. And that set the tone for a desperately turgid opening session. Pretorius launched his Bears career with a promising, pacy spell, well supported by Neil Carter, and the first hour yielded a run every five minutes. Middlesex crawled to 13 from 13 overs before the 14th over at last threw up a thrill. Koenig edged Alan Richardson to second slip where Mark Wagh wrapped cold hands round the ball.

As the attrition continued in front of a couple of hundred spectators shivering among more than 20,000 empty seats, it was forgivable to suspect that the nation is not entirely gripped by the birth of a new county season. And therefore to think perhaps county cricket, or at least the county championship, really is the anachronism some make it out to be.

v. Middlesex at Edgbaston

But that is, of course, such an easy trap into which to fall. Edgbaston was virtually empty today, yes, but then there were the legions calling up Ceefax and Cricinfo for the score. Or tuning into the radio or picking up the evening paper for details of the action that they simply cannot, due to work, school, family commitments, ill-health or imprisonment, witness. County cricket remains a massive latent presence in English sporting life.

So, watched by few but monitored by millions, Middlesex ground on. Batsmen watched carefully and defended. Bowlers reacquainted stiff muscles with the motions required by their art and tried to land the ball on the cut strip. Fielders rubbed their hands and tunnelled them into trouser pockets and thanked the Lord for that heroic, long-mourned 17th-century cricketer's wife, almost certainly an antecedent of the Graces, who first conceived, designed and knitted the chunky sweater.

Action-wise, things perked up a bit after lunch. Dougie Brown's arrival in the attack usually triggers activity and sure enough he soon lured Owais Shah into an edge to Wagh at second slip. For a few momentous minutes Wagh was on target for an incredible record - to take every single catch pouched by Warwickshire in a county season. But then Ben Hutton, after 107 minutes of defiance, wafted at Brown and wicket-keeper Tony Frost accepted his first catch of the season, the 117th of his first-class career.

Action. Movement. Middlesex 69 for three and, with Warwickshire on top, if the ground was not quite a cauldron of noise, at least it felt as though the season had begun. Ed Joyce and Paul Weekes dug in until, at twenty past three, the realisation dawned that the clammy murk in which the players had been moving about for some time was in fact significant drizzle. Off they went.

And off they stayed. Members headed for the bar. In the dressing-room the cards came out and on went Ceefax for news from Bristol, Northampton and The Oval. Finally, at 5.20pm, umpires Neil Mallender and George Sharp stuck their noble former Northamptonshire beaks out of the pavilion one last time to confirm that it was still inclement. Home time. Season underway in an aqueous, staccato sort of way.

The Year of the Bear

Saturday, April 17th:

Middlesex 432 for 8 declared
Warwickshire 16 for 1

Just like every season, except 2000 and 2001 when they competed in the Second Division, Warwickshire started this one aiming to win the county championship. Only five times - 1911, 1951, 1972, 1994 and 1995 - since 1895 have they managed to do that and the chances of making it six this time round are, on the evidence of today, slimmer than a cream-cracker.

In overcast, bowler-friendly conditions this morning, Neil Carter quickly sent back Ed Joyce for 39 to leave Middlesex 119 for four and vulnerable. Further breakthroughs then and a decent foundation for only the Bears' 32nd victory in 121 first-class matches against the London county (Middlesex have won 42) would be in place. Instead Middlesex ended up declaring half an hour before the close on a handsome 432 for eight - and then did immediate damage to Warwickshire's reply.

Paul Weekes and James Dalrymple were the rocks on which a toiling Bears bowling attack floundered. The fifth-wicket pair added 175 with considerable panache. Their work quietened the hitherto chirpy Bears and entered the record books as Middlesex's highest fifth-wicket offering against Warwickshire at the expense of young Jack Hearne and the belligerent Frank Mann whose partnership of 171 graced this very plot 75 years ago.

Dalrymple was especially fluent, collecting 52 of his 77 runs in boundaries which included a four and six hooked from successive balls from Pretorius. Weekes applied his customary cussed approach to accumulate 118 in four hours 26 minutes during which Knight, in his first match as captain, rotated eight bowlers like a man embarking on a jigsaw by rummaging in the box for the corners to start him off.

Brown finally bowled Weekes but heads were dropping by the time David Nash helped himself to 55 after tea. To rub salt in the wounds, Melvyn Betts got his snout in the trough too. Making his Middlesex debut after being released by Warwickshire last

v. Middlesex at Edgbaston

autumn, Betts flailed away for 31 from 40 balls to lift his team over 400.

Only Brad Hogg, who snared his first Warwickshire wicket when Simon Cook fell lbw, and Brown emerged with much credit before Shah declared to leave the Bears five overs batting. Chad Keegan promptly produced a rapid in-ducker to have Knight lbw and round off a poor day at the office for the new captain and his team.

Sunday, April 18th: No play

Rain. Ever since 1885 when Lord Calthorpe offered a parcel of "rough grazing land" in Edgbaston to Warwickshire to end their search for a proper base in Birmingham, it's been dropping by on a pretty regular basis.

Take 1888 for example. In only their third season at the sparkling new ground the Bears, still to be designated a first-class county, had mighty Yorkshire reeling only for Lord Hawke's men to be helped off the hook by a downpour (just as they had been when the two teams met at Halifax earlier that summer). That damned rain.

Then there was 1902: Australia sensationally rattled all out for 36 by George Hirst and Wilfred Rhodes in the inaugural Test at Edgbaston only for England to be robbed of victory by a deluge from above. What about August 21, 1928? A vast Tuesday crowd gathered to watch the final day of Warwickshire's tussle with Hampshire, fascinatingly poised with the visiting side set to resume 138 runs ahead with seven wickets down and the wicket turning. Tantalising - only for rain to wipe out the denouement. Or 46 years later when Surrey visited Edgbaston in mid-August and found their former player Bob Willis fired up to make a few points. Willis sent back one, two and three Mike Edwards, Lonsdale Skinner and Geoff Howarth in the space of 10 balls and Surrey were 19 for three with Willis closing in on an historic all-ten with 5.3-4-3-3 when the final day was washed out. Cruel. Bleedin' rain.

Now add Sunday April 18, 2004 to the list. Not much rain fell during the day itself but plenty dropped on Birmingham in the preceding 12 hours so parts of the field, most notably the bowlers' run-ups at the Pavilion End, were deemed unsafe.

The Year of the Bear

Several inspections took place with the umpires and captains tiptoeing gingerly round the covers, glancing glumly skyward, hitching up their trousers and shaking their heads. The cause was deemed hopeless in mid-afternoon. Too wet. Not safe. Quite unreasonable and irresponsible to ask these finely-honed athletes to risk life and limb in such treacherous conditions.

Minutes after play was abandoned Warwickshire's players emerged from the pavilion for a game of football on the outfield. Strange.

Monday, April 19:

Warwickshire 317
Middlesex 54 for 2 declared
Warwickshire 24 for 0

MATCH DRAWN:
WARWICKSHIRE 9 POINTS, MIDDLESEX 12

If this match was to be steered out of a cul-de-sac the captains had to collude this morning. They didn't, so up a cul-de-sac it determinedly, greyly and finally bizarrely spent the day heading.

Morning entertainment came from Betts' first bowl for his new county. The former Durham seamer is recalled at Edgbaston as an under-achiever - brisk and effective when the mood took him but horribly loose and expensive when it didn't. And the mood didn't take him anywhere near often enough. And it didn't today.

It's hard to believe Betts wasn't up for it against the county which recently discarded him but his figures of 8-0-74-0 tell the story. Betts threw open the doors of the Pavilion End Cafeteria and richly did Wagh and Trott feast on a banquet of half-volleys and long-hops. The dross from Betts released the pressure after Warwickshire lost Ian Bell, edging Nantie Hayward to slip, to teeter on an uneasy 27 for two. Wagh timed the ball lusciously through the leg-side in his 78 while his partner was more brutal. Trott survived one or two hairy moments against Hayward to strike 13 fours, many punched savagely though the off-side, in an assertive 67 from only 88 balls.

v. Middlesex at Edgbaston

Wagh looked set to start the season with a century until he tickled a leg-side catch to wicket-keeper Nash off Weekes. The off-spinner then sent back Trott, caught off bat-pad, and Troughton, driving loosely to extra cover, soon after lunch but Brown and Hogg averted a collapse. These two were born 12,000 miles apart but are united by a streak of defiance common to many of their countrymen and they appeared to relish batting with a like-minded soul. While Brown got his nut down, Hogg adorned a sombre afternoon with some lovely strokes. Of their first 50 runs added, the Australian's share was 41 and when he perished lbw to the persevering Weekes he had christened his Bears career with 51 from 42 balls with nine fours. Brown plodded on to get a couple of hours batting under his belt for 42. The rest was pretty desultory. Warwickshire 317 all out.

Now came Bell's big chance. With Pretorius ill and Richardson injured, the youngster shared the new ball with Carter. Many fine bowlers - Jack Shilton, Frank Field, Frank Foster, Percy Jeeves, Harry Howell, Danny Mayer, Charlie Grove, Keith Dollery, Roly Thompson, David Brown, Bob Willis, Steve Perryman, Gladstone Small, Allan Donald and others - have propelled the new cherry for Warwickshire County Cricket Club down the years and now Bell is fully entitled to add his name to the list. His five overs, for just eight runs, needed careful watching too. Safe to say he has left his imprint on the Middlesex batting psyche.

The final throes of this shapeless opening fixture were plain silly. Rather than adopt the traditional route on the final day of a dead game and terminate it as quickly as possible, the captains stretched this one out on the rack. Middlesex declared at 54 for two, setting the Bears a target of 170 in five overs. They didn't go for it.

****

The Year of the Bear

SCORECARD

Middlesex first innings

SG Koenig	c Wagh	b Richardson	10
BL Hutton	c Frost	b Brown	30
*OA Shah	c Wagh	b Brown	17
EC Joyce	c Frost	b Carter	39
PN Weekes		b Brown	118
JWM Dalrymple	c Bell	b Pretorius	77
+DC Nash	st Frost	b Wagh	55
SJ Cook	lbw	b Hogg	22
MM Betts	not out		31
Extras	(b 3, lb 10, w 2, nb 18)		33
		Total	**432**
			for 8 dec

CB Keegan and M Hayward did not bat.

FoW: 17, 52, 69, 119, 294, 337, 373, 432.

Pretorius 20-5-95-1, Carter 20-5-59-1, Brown 25-7-65-3, Richardson 24-4-92-1, Bell 2-0-10-0, Hogg 22-5-45-1, Trott 3-0-22-0, Wagh 8.2-0-31-1.

Warwickshire first innings

*NV Knight	lbw	b Keegan	4
MA Wagh	c Nash	b Weekes	78
IR Bell	c Joyce	b Hayward	12
IJL Trott	c Hutton	b Weekes	67
JO Troughton	c Betts	b Weekes	4
DR Brown		b Hayward	42
GB Hogg	lbw	b Weekes	51
+T Frost	c Nash	b Keegan	4
NM Carter	c Weekes	b Keegan	18
A Richardson	not out		8
D Pretorius		c & b Weekes	1
Extras	(b 2, lb 5, w 3, nb 18)		28
		Total	**317**
			all out

v. Middlesex at Edgbaston

FoW: 8, 27, 157, 167, 204, 272, 283, 303, 312, 317.

Keegan 14-1-63-3, Hayward 14-3-41-2, Betts 8-0-74-0, Cook 14-2-56-0, Weekes 20.4-1-76-5.

Middlesex second innings

SG Koenig	c Frost	b Carter	2
BL Hutton	c Knight	b Trott	20
*OA Shah	not out		20
EC Joyce	not out		10
Extras	(nb 2)		2
		Total	**54**
			for 2 dec

FoW: 12, 27.

Carter 8-3-21-1, Bell 5-2-8-0, Trott 3-1-6-1, Hogg 6-2-15-0, Wagh 1-0-4-0.

Warwickshire second innings

*NV Knight	not out		5
MA Wagh	not out		19
Extras			0
		Total	**24**
			for 0

Nash 2-0-8-0, Joyce 1-0-4-0, Weekes 1-0-5-0, Shah 1-0-7-0

Umpires: NA Mallender and G Sharp.

****

Beat CAMBRIDGE UCCE by 247 runs (friendly).
Lost to HAMPSHIRE by 26 runs (totesport)

Visits to Fenner's used to be valid practice for first-class counties but have long become little more than a net and Warwickshire duly pasted the students by 247 runs. Wagh (105 including a century before lunch) and Frost (80 not out) enjoyed time at the crease but observing the UCCE's batsmen's strokeless attempts to survive was as entertaining as watching a doomed fish slapping about on deck. At least Naqaash Tahir had something to shout about. He collected a wicket with his second ball in first-class cricket when Toby Hembry edged to Frost. Tahir's 13-7-25-2 was full of promise. Hogg's inability to run through the students' mediocre batting was worrying but Nick Knight wanted his team to win and win well and that's what they did.

Four days later the totesport League campaign started in low-key fashion with a 26-run home defeat to Hampshire. Chasing 215 for 6, the Bears folded to 189 all out with only Graham Wagg's three successive sixes off Shane Warne in a lost cause giving the crowd much to cheer.

****

Two

v Gloucestershire
at Edgbaston

Wednesday, April 28th: No play

The Bears' season started against Middlesex with a splutter for sure. And that will only encourage Warwickshire supporters who believe in omens.

Those people will point to 1911 and Warwickshire's glorious inaugural championship triumph - arguably the most sensational success story in the history of world sport - which began with the mother of all splutters. Starting off against Surrey at The Oval the Bears were all out for 62 and 87 and capitulated in little more than a day and a half. Their cricket was described in *Wisden* as "inexcusably weak" but captain Charlie Cowan (a toff with little aptitude for cricket who bagged a pair in the game) immediately made way for Frank Foster and 116 days later, Foster's men were greeted as heroes by thousands thronging New Street station as they returned from clinching the title with victory at Northampton.

Then they - these omen-fanciers, that is - will also flag up 1972. On September 9th that year Warwickshire's players breakfasted on champagne and kippers in their Nottingham hotel having secured the championship with a match to spare. Very Bohemian. But it had all been a bit less celebratory back in April when they started the season by getting turned over by Oxford University. A powerful

29

The Year of the Bear

Bears team including Rohan Kanhai, Mike and Alan Smith, Dennis Amiss and David Brown lost by two wickets at The Parks as Oxford reached a target of 218 in three hours with two balls to spare. That despite Neil Abberley's astute career-best 2 for 19. Red faces. But 134 days later those faces were being filled with champagne and kippers.

And what, those omen-observers then say, about 1995? Fresh from their 1994 treble, the Bears opened up with a friendly against England 'A' at Edgbaston and were battered by an innings and 58 runs. Bob Woolmer's reign as coach ended with a whimper as Phil Neale, in charge of England 'A' one last time before succeeding Woolmer at Edgbaston, supervised his side to victory less than an over into the final day. It was quite a match. Snow fell, hailstones hammered down, Graeme Welch outfoxed Michael Vaughan, Allan Donald supplied Paul Nixon with a broken finger, Min Patel scored a half-century and the Bears were emphatically beaten. Yet they went on to win the title by 32 points.

Oh yes, given those precedents, a crap start can be viewed as a cracking start. On that could John Inverarity and his chaps dwell today as the scheduled opening day against Gloucestershire was washed away. Captains Nick Knight and Chris Taylor were keen to play and three times the covers came off and a start-time was decreed. Each time the rain returned just as David Wainwright was preparing his pens.

Thursday, April 29th: No play

There was never a chance today. After a day and a half of persistent rain the ground was saturated. Although very little rain fell during the scheduled playing time the prospects were always as bleak as the scene, with the pitch and surrounds covered, the scoreboards blank and the massed ranks of seats supplying hospitality to puddles instead of arses.

With the first half of this match washed out, Warwickshire look certain to be kept waiting for a win after their opening two games, both at home. Their season remains stalled.

v. Gloucestershire at Edgbaston

Friday, April 30th:

Gloucestershire 314 for 4

Play at last but still the Bears' season remains stalled. Their cricket today was poor.

Knight won the toss and therefore first use of helpful bowling conditions - moisture in the air and a bit of movement off the pitch. But they were completely wasted by his bowlers. In 80 overs, Gloucestershire plundered 48 fours and three sixes, statistics which, Inverarity was quick to observe post-play, spoke for themselves. The only consolation is that the match is so truncated by rain it can only limp to a draw tomorrow.

Gloucestershire should have had to graft for every run this morning but Craig Spearman and Philip Weston were soon scoring freely without having to take anything remotely resembling a risk. Pretorius and Carter delivered little on a good length and after 40 minutes of play, with the score hurrying along at six per over, an alarmed Knight took the unusual step of calling his team together in a huddle in front of the RES Wyatt Stand.

It was a strong-minded and commendably proactive move by the new skipper but it did not achieve much. (Huddles are overrated. Who can forget Lincoln City's youth team indulging in one seconds before their crunch FA Youth Cup local derby clash with arch-rivals Scunthorpe United at Sincil Bank in 1997? They conceded a goal after 20 seconds and lost 4-0.)

Anyway, out of the huddle came an idea: Bell was brought on. Bad idea as Spearman punched him for five successive fours through the off-side. The strong wind was far from ideal for Bell's drift-based slow-medium - and anyway it's Middlesex who should fear him most grievously.

Spearman galloped to 50 from 39 balls and sped ominously to 77, including 60 in fours, before the Bears enjoyed a pre-lunch bonus. To widespread surprise, the New Zealander imploded by steering Brown carelessly to Hogg at point. Still, Gloucestershire attacked their pasta at 125 for 1 from 22 overs, heights for which they could barely have hoped after losing the toss. Had Taylor called correctly he would have had no hesitation in choosing to field.

Luncheon failed to inspire the Bears. On a blustery, grey afternoon much more suited to rugby league, kite-flying or lighthouse-keeping than cricket, the seamers continued to underperform. Weston defended patiently, content to wait for the next loose offering, and he never had to wait too long. Twice the former Worcestershire man pulled Richardson for six en route to the 20th first-class century of his career. Brown, like Bell earlier in the day, was dispatched for five successive fours. This time Matt Windows was the main beneficiary. He accepted the first four (three to a culpably unprotected third-man fence) before Weston punished the first ball of Brown's next over.

Pretorius came closest to galvanising his side. He was still bending his back late in the day and finally ousted Weston via a mistimed pull and snared Windows with the first ball of his final spell of the day. But Gloucestershire are set fair for maximum batting points and Inverarity and Knight planted some calm and measured, but also stern, words in their team's shell-likes after the close.

Saturday, May 1st:

Gloucestershire 400 for 7 declared.
Warwickshire 139 for 6

MATCH DRAWN.
WARWICKSHIRE 6 POINTS,
GLOUCESTERSHIRE 11

Many times, since he first lumbered onto a championship field on their behalf at Guildford in 1994, have Warwickshire looked to Dougie Brown for inspiration.

Frequently throughout that decade has Brown stirred up a torpid team-display and the 34-year-old insists that he has entered this season, his 13th on the staff at Edgbaston, feeling physically as strong as ever. As for his appetite for cricket - well, Billy Quaife played his last game for Warwickshire at 56 and perhaps Brown will still be chugging in at Edgbaston when the 2025/26 season gets under way.

v. Gloucestershire at Edgbaston

This morning he was out of the traps like a greyhound and inscribed his name onto a very special list. Gloucestershire set off requiring another 86 from 50 overs to claim full batting points but they did not enjoy the stroll of yesterday as Brown struck hard and early. He nipped one way to have Alex Gidman caught behind then, next ball, arrowed one back in to trap Mark Alleyne lbw. When Chris Taylor tickled a catch down the leg-side to Frost, Brown had three wickets without conceding a run but it was Alleyne's dismissal that elevated him on to that list. It was Brown's 400th wicket for the Bears, lifting him alongside Freddie Calthorpe, Tom Cartwright, Frank Foster, Billy Ibadulla, Billy Quaife, Sydney Santall and Bob Wyatt as harvesters of 400 wickets and 6,000 runs for Warwickshire. Brown is up among the county's greats.

He could not dislodge Steve Adshead and Alastair Bressington though. They eased their team to maximum batting points with few alarms and after Gloucestershire's declaration the Bears' untidy match became untidier. Wagh edged a good one first ball from James Averis, then Bell attempted to drive his first ball and also nicked behind to bag a blob of the golden variety. 4 for 2.

Just like the Middlesex game, it was a bad start for the top order and, although not too alarming because both matches were already on a cold slab by the time the batsmen got in, hardly confidence-building stuff. Confidence is however a commodity that Trott, nurtured amid the rabid intensity drilled into school sports teams in South Africa, never lacks and he was soon thrusting away, altering Averis' figures with some fierce drives. Knight knuckled down in search of form and lasted 100 minutes before succumbing to the deserving Lewis. Trott batted 12 minutes less than his captain for 42 more runs before getting a shooter from Bressington.

Then it got tatty again. From 116 for 2, the Bears slid to 139 for 6 as Lewis induced fatal edges from Troughton and Brown, and it was a less than devastating blow when rain returned during the tea interval. Gloucestershire deservedly took the lion's share of bonus points - 11 to the Bears' six - and Inverarity had his thinking cap on. "The players don't need me to tell them they've underperformed," he said. But no doubt he gently pointed it out to them all the same.

The Year of the Bear

Two games, two rain-ruined draws. A slow and at times sloppy start. The silver lining: the clouds that have emptied themselves so freely on Edgbaston have done so just as freely everywhere else too. Or rather not the same clouds - they would have to be exceptionally fast-moving clouds to do that - but others of their ilk. Anyway the bottom line is that the 2004 championship race has begun with a plethora of draws everywhere and Warwickshire's slow start hasn't cost them anything as long as they get their act together sharpish.

****

SCORECARD

Gloucestershire 1st innings

CM Spearman	c Hogg	b Brown	77
WPC Weston	c Richardson	b Pretorius	122
THC Hancock	c Frost	b Carter	44
MGN Windows	c Knight	b Pretorius	48
*CG Taylor	c Frost	b Brown	22
APR Gidman	c Frost	b Brown	1
MW Alleyne	lbw	b Brown	0
+SJ Adshead	not out		56
AN Bressington	not out		19
Extras	(lb 2, w 1, nb 8)		11
		Total	**400**
			for 7 dec

JMM Averis, J Lewis did not bat.

FoW: 1-120, 2-198, 3-296, 4-309, 5-322, 6-322, 7-335.

Pretorius 18-4-69-2, Carter 13-2-57-1, Brown 26-12-75-4, Bell 4-1-34-0, Richardson 14-1-62-0, Hogg 20-5-61-0, Wagh 8.2-0-35-0, Troughton 3-2-5-0.

Warwickshire 1st innings

*NV Knight	lbw	b Lewis	34
MA Wagh	c Adshead	b Averis	0
IR Bell	c Adshead	b Averis	0

v. Gloucestershire at Edgbaston

IJL Trott		b Bressington	76
JO Troughton	c Adshead	b Lewis	14
DR Brown	c Alleyne	b Lewis	0
OGB Hogg	not out		8
+T Frost	not out		0
Extras	(lb 3, nb 4)		7
		Total	**139**
			for 6

NM Carter, A Richardson and D Pretorius did not bat.

FoW: 1-4, 2-4, 3-116, 4-120, 5-124, 6-139.

Lewis 12-5-21-3, Averis 7-0-40-2, Gidman 5-0-31-0, Bressington 6-0-38-1, Alleyne 3-2-6-0.

Umpires: JW Holder and VA Holder.

****

The Year of the Bear

Lost to ESSEX by 6 runs (totesport),
Beat SHROPSHIRE by 8 wickets (C&G Trophy),
Beat SURREY by 45 runs (totesport).

Next came three one-dayers. A totesport League visit to Chelmsford brought a narrow defeat in a late-evening 10-over thrash. The field was soaked (Pretorius was surprised to find himself fielding in a puddle at third-man) but the Sky cameras were present so cricket there had to be. If only that sort of enterprise was always shown! A classy unbeaten 40 from 21 balls by Nasser Hussain, in his last innings against the Bears, lifted Essex to 89 for 2, a target which Warwickshire, fiddling with the batting order, did not threaten as much the narrow margin suggests.

Back at base, after a cruise past Shropshire in the C&G Trophy, the Bears opened their totesport League points tally at the third attempt. They amassed 240 against Surrey who promptly collapsed to 7 for 4, three early wickets falling to Pretorius who ended with 4 for 36. Without a victory of any kind this season, humiliated by Ireland in the C&G and with personality conflicts affecting the camp, Surrey are next up at Edgbaston in the championship. A top-class crew including three of England's best batsmen of their generation - Mark Butcher, Graham Thorpe and Mark Ramprakash - arrive aboard an unhappy ship. Should be intriguing.

****

Three

v Surrey
at Edgbaston

Wednesday, May 12th:

Warwickshire 358 for 6

A bit like the old days, this. A county championship match brimming with top players.

It used to be like this all the time. The prestige domestic competition pitting champions of the sport against each other and, down the years, as much as ever when Surrey and Warwickshire have met. Tom Richardson tearing in at Herbert Bainbridge. Frank Foster trying to ruffle the peerless Jack Hobbs. Bob Wyatt watching for every cunning variation from Alf Gover. Lance Gibbs probing away to outwit the adamantine Kenny Barrington. As recently as the 1970s, the Edgbaston regulars watched a Bears side including Dennis Amiss, John Jameson and David Brown of England and Rohan Kanhai of West Indies face a Surrey team including John Edrich, Graham Roope, Geoff Arnold and Pat Pocock of England, Geoff Howarth of New Zealand and Younis Ahmed of Pakistan. Great duels. Great times.

And times largely lost. Now international cricket has become so all-consuming, so all-important and so all-bleedin'-year-round that its stars are rested. Deemed too precious to risk life and limb in the crazy, madcap, health-threatening maelstrom that is county cricket, they are ordered to lie low. But here we have a throwback.

The Year of the Bear

To a Warwickshire side including former, present or future internationals Nick Knight, Dougie Brown, Brad Hogg, Jim Troughton, Dewald Pretorius and Ian Bell is added the esteemed name of Ashley Giles. An exotic bird this Giles, rarely glimpsed flitting, sylph-like, round the Edgbaston turf since the advent of central contracts. But Giles has been uncaged by England coach Duncan Fletcher for this game to get some overs in. He bowled only 23 during England's pace-dominated Test series triumph in the Caribbean in the winter.

In Surrey's XI, meanwhile, lurk nine internationals - only opening batsman Scott Newman and skipper Jon Batty have not played at the highest level. It's a line-up soaked with class and experience but Batty has arrived in Birmingham with problems. His appointment as captain during the winter did not meet with universal approval from senior players and there are whispers of whispers in the dressing room. So far in 2004 the team's accomplished parts have amounted to a grumpy and dishevelled whole.

Both teams need to crank their season into gear in this match and with the sun at last deigning to shine on the fledgling season there was a decent crowd in for a Wednesday morning. Knight's excellent form with the toss continued - that's three won out of three in the champo - and he chose to bat on a good-looking pitch. But again those top-order gremlins surfaced.

After Wagh sliced into the slips, Knight and Bell added 50 but then perished in quick succession to Saqlain Mushtaq, who was already obtaining spin before lunch. Knight edged one that turned big on him before Bell departed in infuriating fashion. He looked in great nick for 34 from 59 balls but then chipped the ball down the throat of Ramprakash at mid-wicket. At 71 for 3, after the top-order twitches of the first two matches, there were grumbles among the members and growing suspicions of a glass chin to Warwickshire's much-vaunted batting order.

Shoring up was required - and the middle-order responded brilliantly. Troughton enjoyed an early reprieve - the left-hander had only three when Adam Hollioake grassed a slip chance off James Ormond - and Surrey bowled intelligently to deny him the width he relishes. But he remained patient and, with the resolute

Trott, rebuilt the innings. They added 119 with increasing conviction and after Trott departed (for 61 from 101 balls - his third successive half-century) shaking his head and glowering at an lbw decision, Brown settled in. And after Troughton, having just lifted Salisbury for six, departed (for 77 from 166 balls) attempting to repeat the shot, Hogg settled in.

Hogg did more than settle in, in fact. Straight away the left-hander took the game to Surrey and the initiative away from them. He was down the wicket and in their faces from his first ball faced and needed only a further 47 before his ninth four took him to 50.

Hogg and Brown added 64 and after Brown's 131-minute stay was ended by Martin Bicknell, Giles settled in. By the close, the early menace of Saqlain had been well and truly subdued and Warwickshire, with Hogg on 69 and Giles 17, had enjoyed their first good day of the season.

Thursday, May 13th:

Warwickshire 546 Surrey 190 for 7

If Wednesday was a good day, then how about this? Surrey, for all their Test stars, are on the rack and resembling a rabble.

Safe to say that Hogg has endeared himself to the notoriously hard-to-please Warwickshire regulars. Some of that lot make the hecklers at the Glasgow Empire seem as amiable as the Bracebridge Heath Knitting Centre Summer Flower Show's tombola committee, but they had no complaints this morning as Hogg resumed where he left off last night, cutting, pulling and driving rapaciously.

Troubles crowded in for Batty. Just when he needed his main men right beside him, Saqlain stayed in the pavilion nursing a knee injury. Without his trump card the captain shuffled his pack with increasing desperation from behind the stumps as Hogg and Giles filled their boots.

Hogg was soon lifting his bat towards the dressing room to acknowledge only the third first-class century of his career - and the first for 10 years. Giles, meanwhile, happily fed upon the surfeit of wide and overpitched offerings that came his way and the pair posted 191 from only 40 overs. It is Warwickshire's record seventh-wicket stand against Surrey, surpassing the 170 lodged by Alan Smith and Tom Cartwright who so skilfully drew the sting of Peter Loader and David Gibson after they had reduced the Bears to 44 for 6 at The Oval in 1961.

Giles returned to Bears' colours with a sterling 70 from 126 balls - his 22nd time past 50 in first-class cricket - but to Hogg will go the headlines. His 158 occupied just 163 balls (with 19 fours and a six) and stretched Surrey's fragile morale to breaking point. A standing ovation accompanied him to the pavilion where there were no doubt a few knowing smiles in the offices of those who backed the decision to hire him. In three championship innings so far Hogg has scored 217 for twice out from 224 balls with 30 fours and a six. If he can get among the wickets too, the Bears have made a hell of a signing.

Having squandered a first-morning position of high promise Surrey were really not in the mood for a spot of thrashing by Carter. But weary from more than 130 overs in the field, they were vulnerable to it and, much to the crowd's delight, that's what came next. Carter's 29 from 22 balls hoisted the Bears well beyond 500. Even Pretorius twisted the knife by doubling his previous best for the Bears. His fluent unbeaten two (six balls, seven minutes, no fours) extended the total to 546, a Warwickshire record at home to Surrey. Banished from the roll of honour was the 1906 team which punished Surrey for 510 here thanks largely to John Devey scoring a century - a nifty move from the former Aston Villa captain in his own benefit game. Rapidly did the hats (it's buckets nowadays - how technology marches on!) fill up when the collectors circulated the ground.

The suffering of Surrey circa 2004 was far from over. They had only two runs on the board when Carter surprised Butcher with bounce and the England man gloved to Bell at short leg. Newman, batting as if in Twenty20 rather than gazing up at a follow-on figure of 397, sped to 28 then flashed fatally at a wide one from Pretorius. Carter bowled with a purpose which suggested he has fully taken on board the coach's demand for more from him this season, and unleashed another fine delivery that Ramprakash edged into the slips. 50 for 3 and that 397 was a distant speck on the horizon.

v. Surrey at Edgbaston

Batty and Thorpe applied themselves. Thorpe reached 13 before he was confronted by his close buddy Giles. The spinner found his mate's outside-edge in his first over but Frost failed to cling on. Never mind. "Let the little ones go," the great Somerset slip catcher Len Braund once said. And while Thorpe does not normally constitute a little one, this drop proved inexpensive as he soon top-edged a sweep at Wagh and this time Frost made no mistake. Three balls later Surrey were 98 for 5 after Hollioake had driven a return catch to Wagh. Thought-bubbles above the heads of the departing Hollioake and Batty, leaning on his bat at the Pavilion End as his former leader passed by, would have made interesting reading.

With Giles looking a bit rusty and Hogg struggling for control, Wagh did not suffer at all in comparison. Troughton also got a bowl to make it a four-pronged spin armoury but the admirable Batty defended as though his life depended upon it. He lost two more partners, both to dozy shots, after tea. Azhar Mahmood bizarrely offered no stroke to a straight full-length ball from Hogg and Bicknell missed a Giles full toss. Both were dispatched lbw and Surrey closed 207 short of the follow-on figure with only three wickets to fall. In dominoes terms the Bears are entering the final straight with a full hand of sixes with Surrey still just finishing the first lap.

Friday, May 14th:

Surrey 302 and 243 for 2

Now this was truly like the old days. Not just top players playing but a morning session consisting of 49 overs of spin. Fascinating cricket. Like mother used to make.

Professional pride kicked in for Surrey after their dire work yesterday. At last this morning Batty found, in Ian Salisbury, a colleague also determined to sell his wicket dearly. They saw off Giles, still short of rhythm, and Hogg, still lacking accuracy, so Wagh and Troughton took up the attack, the latter with a degree of control that suggested there's plenty of value to come from his slow left arm.

The Year of the Bear

But Batty stretched his resistance into its fourth hour. Implacably watchful, only once, with a slog-sweep for six off Hogg, did he cast aside caution. Salisbury's simple technique served him well until, in the day's 40th over, he was deceived by a quicker one from Giles and adjudged lbw. At two hours six minutes for 34 runs, an innings of aesthetic beauty it wasn't but Salisbury grafted diligently for his team. That was something of which Ormond could not be accused as he swatted Giles carelessly to mid-off.

Enter Saqlain with a runner. Twenty-two minutes later they made the return journey after the Pakistani bat-padded off Hogg to give the Aussie 2 for 87 in 24 overs without a maiden. Batty narrowly missed out on the century he richly deserved. The captain remained unbeaten on 92 after five hours and 26 minutes of intense concentration. He faced 313 balls, only seven of which went for four.

When Surrey followed on, Batty (who in 1996, it shouldn't be forgotten, helped Walsall to a magnificent Birmingham League and Abbot Ale Cup double - have any of his illustrious teammates got that on their CV?) could only hope his example would focus a few minds among his errant flock second time round. At the end of the third day the evidence is that it did. Surrey set off needing 244 to avoid an innings defeat and by the close had acquired 243 of them with just two men out. Butcher was the driving force. He survived a colossal lbw shout from Carter first ball but thereafter batted beautifully, no doubt to the satisfaction of watching England selectors David Graveney and Rodney Marsh. The spinners were soon wheeling away but to little avail. The pitch has not worn as expected. With Butcher's timing and placement, particularly on the off-side, of the highest quality, Warwickshire could only hope the other end proved more fragile. It did, eventually. Newman passed 50 with six from a Hogg full-toss but then top-edged a big sweep at Wagh and Knight moved under the catch from slip.

Out strode Ramprakash with an ocean of runs against Warwickshire already behind him in his long career. The Bears sensed that Ramprakash was trouble from the moment he first faced them as a 17-year-old college student on a damp Friday afternoon at Uxbridge in 1987. That late-August day, at the end of a rain-affected contest in north London, he nonchalantly negated the best efforts of Gladstone Small, Tony Merrick, Norman Gifford, Tim Munton and Asif Din to see Middlesex safely to a draw - and he's been a pain in the Bears' butt ever since. And the older he gets the bigger the pain: 88 not out and 120 not out against them for Middlesex in 2000, then having not faced them in 2001, 99 and 210 not out for Surrey in 2002 and 182 not out at Edgbaston last year.

Another big 'un appeared to be nigh when he motored to 35 (including a six swept off Wagh into the Hollies Stand) at almost a-run-a-ball but then a big surprise. Ramprakash's first error proved his last when an attempt to lift Giles straight found only the hands of Pretorius.

Big surprise. Big blow. But out came another big name. Thorpe joined Butcher to see it through to the close with ominous assurance. With shadows lengthening in the evening sunshine, butterflies chasing each other above the dormant slip cordon, the River Rea trickling insouciantly by and a skein of geese curving away in the direction of the Custard Factory, Butcher made the most elegant progress to 100 from 160 balls. He reached stumps on 114 looking for all the world as though he fancies batting all day tomorrow - and is capable of it. The Bears have bossed this game all the way through but still need a big push on the final day.

Saturday, May 15th:

Surrey 414. Warwickshire 171 for 3.

WARWICKSHIRE WON BY SEVEN WICKETS. WARWICKSHIRE 22 POINTS, SURREY 5.

It's very early days yet. And nobody in the history of sport is a more devout follower of the take-each-game-as-it-comes theory than Nicholas Verity Knight. But if Warwickshire can produce astounding sessions of cricket like they did between lunch and tea today then anything's possible this season.

For almost two hours this morning Butcher and Thorpe continued to bat beautifully. There was a good crowd in on a lovely Saturday morning - bright and warm - but their hopes of an early breakthrough were thwarted by two high-class batsmen playing with discipline and no little flair. With lunch approaching and Butcher closing in on a double century and Thorpe on the verge of a century, a draw looked odds-on.

But the Bears' heads stayed up. They were picked off for occasional boundaries but never let the run-rate escape control. Accompanied, as ever, by fulsome exhortations from the voluble Frost and Trott - the Hinge and Brackett of county cricket - they kept at it. Still time was running out fast when the third-wicket partnership reached 178 and Surrey, at 364 for 2, were 120 ahead with eight wickets in hand and just over two sessions left. And the pitch, far from deteriorating, was played better the longer the match went on.

With the possessors of a combined 10,000 Test runs at the crease and set there as if in stone, something special was required. Warwickshire, who of course not only had to take the wickets but then chase the runs, needed a big push with the second new ball. Something special? How about sweeping away the last eight wickets for 50 runs?

Pretorius took the new cherry from the Pavilion End, pitched it up and watched with delight as it swung to take the outside-edge and terminate Thorpe's resistance at three minutes short of three hours. A glimmer of hope.

In went Batty. If he took root again it was a draw for sure. But Pretorius had a head of steam up. He beat the Surrey captain for pace and the bails flew like sparks. The glimmer was starting to brighten...then suddenly it was aflame after Butcher's feet, for once, got in a tangle and Pretorius bowled him off the inside-edge. The left-hander was gone for 184 from 331 balls with 22 fours in six hours two minutes. Perhaps sensing what was to follow, he sagged back to the pavilion.

The Bears, on the other hand, were buoyant. Now Carter, charging in from the City End, struck hard. A spiteful lifter sent Hollioake on his way for a pair. Mahmood and Salisbury both edged fecklessly into the slip-cordon to roars from spectators who were starting to realise that an amazing session was unfolding in front of their very peepers. Surrey had folded from 364 for 2 to 395 for 8.

v. Surrey at Edgbaston

When Bicknell was castled by Brown, Knight showed his steely streak. Last man Saqlain hobbled out with Hollioake as a runner but the Bears' captain intervened gently but firmly to send the latter back to the pavilion. If Saqqy was fit enough to deliver 32 overs, Knight reasoned, he could surely manage to limp up and down 22 yards if necessary. Poor Hollioake, already dismissed for a pair, was banished fruitlessly to the dressing room for the third time in the match.

Saqlain's knee was not to be further distressed. The spinner survived two balls then played round a straight one and a staggering collapse was complete. The figures of Carter and Pretorius might not look much but they had bowled magnificently. Rarely can figures have done less justice to a bowler's impact on a match than Pretorius' 18-2-88-3.

There was still work to do. A target of 171 in 41 overs was no formality and with Surrey, even this moody incarnation of them, you never know. Knight took Carter out with him in the hope of a bit of productive, pressure-easing pinch-hitting and the left-hander's 24 from 26 balls did the job nicely. Wagh's contribution of 12 was small but, consisting of three boundaries in an over, continued the momentum perfectly.

All the time Knight worked the ball around adroitly and he found two perfect partners in Bell and Trott. Bell's busy 31 spanned only 47 balls and after he was bowled by Saqlain, Trott made his intentions clear by immediately dancing down the wicket to drive the Pakistani. Trott had reached 35 from only 29 balls and Knight had played himself nicely into form with an unbeaten 62 from 85 when the target was reached with startling comfort with 49 balls to spare.

A fantastic day's cricket by Warwickshire to complete a fantastic victory. A really good all-round performance; record-breaking batting, big-hearted bowling, aggressive fielding. And, from nowhere, the Bears are right up in the thick of the First Division leaders.

****

45

The Year of the Bear

SCORECARD

Warwickshire 1st innings

*NV Knight	c Batty	b Saqlain	28
MA Wagh	c A. Mahmood	b Ormond	0
IR Bell	c Ramprakash	b Saqlain	34
IJL Trott	lbw	b Saqlain	61
JO Troughton	st Batty	b Salisbury	77
DR Brown	c Ramprakash	b Bicknell	44
GB Hogg	c Batty	b Bicknell	158
AF Giles	c A. Mahmood	b Salisbury	70
+T Frost	c Batty	b Bicknell	10
NM Carter	c Ramprakash	b Bicknell	29
D Pretorius	not out		2
Extras	(b 11, lb 13, nb 9)		33
		Total	**546**
			all out

FoW: 1-14, 2-64, 3-71, 4-190, 5-242, 6-306, 7-497, 8-505, 9-544, 10-546.

Bicknell 27.3-5-130-4, Ormond 29-2-103-1, Saqlain Mushtaq 32-5-77-3, Azhar Mahmood 20-4-94-0, Salisbury 32-8-97-2, Hollioake 4-0-21-0.

Surrey 1st innings

SA Newman	c Frost	b Pretorius	2
MA Butcher	c Bell	b Carter	0
MR Ramprakash	c Wagh	b Carter	11
GP Thorpe	c Frost	b Wagh	4
*+JN Batty	not out		92
AJ Hollioake		c & b Wagh	0
Azhar Mahmood	lbw	b Hogg	27
MP Bicknell	lbw	b Giles	37
IDK Salisbury	lbw	b Giles	3
J Ormond	c Carter	b Giles	4
Saqlain Mushtaq	c Brown	b Hogg	14
Extras	(lb 8, w 5)		13
		Total	**302**
			all out

v. Surrey at Edgbaston

FoW: 1-2, 2-32, 3-50, 4-98, 5-98, 6-133, 7-183, 8-267, 9-275, 10-302 .

Pretorius 11-2-47-1, Carter 9-5-22-2, Giles 35-13-55-3, Brown 4-0-14-0, Wagh 26-9-60-2, Hogg 24-0-87-2, Troughton 13-5-9-0.

Surrey 2nd innings (following on)

SA Newman	c Knight	b Wagh	55
MA Butcher		b Pretorius	184
MR Ramprakash	c Pretorius	b Giles	35
GP Thorpe	c Frost	b Pretorius	89
*+JN Batty		b Pretorius	8
AJ Hollioake	c Frost	b Carter	0
Azhar Mahmood	c Knight	b Carter	7
MP Bicknell		b Brown	21
IDK Salisbury	c Wagh	b Carter	0
J Ormond	not out		3
Saqlain Mushtaq	lbw	b Brown	0
Extras	(b 5, lb 7)		12
		Total	**414**
			all out

FoW: 1-124, 2-186, 3-364, 4-382, 5-383, 6-387, 7-395, 8-395, 9-414, 10-414.

Pretorius 18-2-88-3, Carter 14-2-39-3, Bell 3-1-10-0, Giles 27-4-73-1, Brown 15.3-3-40-2, Hogg 18-2-65-0, Wagh 18-2-69-1, Troughton 6-0-18-0.

Warwickshire 2nd innings (target: 171)

NM Carter	run out		24
*NV Knight	not out		62
MA Wagh	lbw	b Saqlain	12
IR Bell		b Saqlain	31
IJL Trott	not out		35
Extras	(b 2, lb 3, nb 2)		7
		Total	**171**
			for 3

JO Troughton, DR Brown, GB Hogg, +T Frost, AF Giles and D Pretorius did not bat.

The Year of the Bear

FoW: 1-47, 2-64, 3-114.

Bicknell 8-0-37-0, Ormond 4-0-30-0, Saqlain Mushtaq 12-1-49-2, Azhar Mahmood 1-0-6-0, Salisbury 7.5-0-44-0.

Umpires: JW Holder and NJ Llong.

****

Four

v Sussex
at Horsham

Wednesday, May 19th:

Warwickshire 357 for 6

With the greatest respect to Crawley, few people arrive here with a spring in their step and joy in their hearts. It's image as a functional, characterless new town is not entirely justified - far from new, parts of the settlement date back to the 12th century. But it's fair to say that most of Crawley's heritage has been engulfed by the engineering works, plastics factories, food-processing plants and traffic islands that arrived as part of the package of 'new town' status just after the Second World War.

Few people unpack their togs in Crawley at the start of a holiday of a lifetime or check in there for their dream honeymoon. It's not that sort of place. But Warwickshire's players checked into the Holiday Inn Crawley last night with a spring in their step and joy in their hearts after sweeping away Surrey in such style.

They unpacked in Crawley because Horsham, where they are playing Sussex, does not contain a hotel with sufficient rooms to accommodate a professional cricket team with its vast retinue of coaches, medical staff, scorer, bag-carriers, chauffeurs and grape-peelers (actually I just made those last three up - Warwickshire's players, even the capped ones, have to carry their own bags, drive their own cars and peel their own grapes). So to

The Year of the Bear

Crawley, a few miles to the north-east, and a hotel overlooking a nice, scenic major traffic island directly underneath a main flight-path to nearby Gatwick Airport - ah the glamour of professional cricket.

The Bears couldn't wait to get to Horsham Cricket Club's pretty Cricketfield Road ground on this sunny but breezy midweek morning and get cracking against the reigning champions. They arrived without Giles. He has joined up with England for the first Test against New Zealand at Lord's although Richardson will drop out tomorrow if Giles is omitted from the Test XI and makes the short hop here.

As the players loosened up before play in nets plonked on the outfield, the atmosphere of the archetypal English outground was unmistakeable. Gorgeous. So serene with the marquees and rows of trees and small pavilion and the scorers operating from a caravan and tennis players knocking up at long-on and members settling into their seats, unscrewing their flasks, passing round the liquorice allsorts and discussing weighty issues such as a) will it stay fine? b) will Sussex retain their title? and, in the case of two distinguished-looking elderly gentleman, immaculate in blazers and ties, the eternal question of ornithological genetics, c) is it possible to breed a pink canary? The big stadia have the kudos and grandeur but at venues like Horsham are county cricket's roots just as deep. The locals are chuffed to bits to have the county side here and if the players have to, in 21st century terms, rough it a bit then so be it. Counties retreat exclusively to their headquarters at their peril.

Sussex, to their great credit, have never shirked from travelling round their patch. Over the years they've played Warwickshire at Hastings, Chichester, Eastbourne, Horsham and Worthing as well as at their Hove HQ. They realise county cricket can't afford to disconnect itself from any followers.

Horsham-wise, it's safe to say that batsmen look forward to their visits more than bowlers. It's always a good track here, although offering turn. Mushtaq Ahmed enjoyed himself here last season when his 12 for 244 engineered Sussex's 10-wicket win over Nottinghamshire. They were the best figures by a Sussex spinner since Eddie Hemmings' 12 for 58 against Leicestershire in 1993 -

v. Sussex at Horsham

also at Horsham! It was here too that George Cox lodged the best match figures by any Sussex bowler on their own patch against Warwickshire - 17 for 106 in 1926. Cox was 52 at the time! Seamers might dread Horsham but twirlers like it here.

So the Hogg, Wagh, Troughton trinity will get their chance. But later because Knight, to his enormous delight, again won the toss and, of course, batted. Enormous delight did not describe his mood an hour later after he played on to Mohammad Akram and missed out on a big 'un. And if there had been a big yellow "I've missed out" paddling-pool situated behind the portaloos to the right of the pavilion at this elegant ground, in which batsmen who have missed out had to go and stand for the rest of the day, Knight would have had plenty of company. Warwickshire were 166 for 5 after Wagh edged an airy drive, Trott missed a sweep, Troughton was bamboozled by Mushtaq and Brown bat-padded.

The champions were right on top. But watching from the other end while his team-mates imploded was Ian Bell. Others came and went within the hour (Knight batted 50 minutes, Wagh 37, Trott 55, Troughton 51, Brown 28) but Bell quietly set down roots and waited for a durable colleague. Hogg provided one.

If it's possible for the flow of a day to hinge on one ball then today's did. Hogg took guard at 166 for 5 with Sussex chirping at the prospect of Mushtaq, with three wickets already, having a serious dart at Cox's record. The maestro was spinning his web and once that started to happen, victim after victim was invariably snared.

Well Hogg didn't see it that way. Rather than flap into the web like a hapless, fragile snipe fly and meekly succumb, he favoured the approach of the big fat bluebottle and powered through it leaving a great big hole and an aggrieved predator. To his very first ball, Hogg was down the wicket biffing Mushy to the mid-on boundary. In that instant Sussex's stranglehold was loosened. While Hogg asserted himself, even more impressive was Bell's technique against the Pakistani. The 22-year-old's shot selection and concentration were beyond criticism in a perfect anchor role.

Sussex didn't help themselves when Hogg, on 22, escaped a leg-side chance to wicket-keeper Tim Ambrose off Akram. It was costly. When, an hour later, Chris Adams clung on to a slip catch to send Hogg on his way for 68 from 101 balls, the partnership was

51

worth 145 in 38 overs. It is a Bears sixth-wicket record against Sussex, surpassing the 137 recorded by those two greats Billy Quaife and Tiger Smith at Hastings in 1914 (when Cox, then a callow 41 had to be content with a modest 9-0-24-0).

Hogg batted beautifully but it was Bell's day. When he reached a flawless century - his first for a year - from 230 balls it was clear how much it meant both to him, as he punched the air, and to his applauding team-mates. In the final hour Frost supplied Bell with further stout support and the pair closed on 14 and 147 respectively. A terrific recovery.

Sussex ended the day reflecting upon a boat missed. Akram's frustrations had been taken out on the ball with which he was deemed by the umpires to have tampered, at a cost of five penalty runs. This adjustment to the score, which took place during the tea interval, completely eluded the occupants of the press-tent until a reporter was enlightened by chance via a conversation overheard in the Gents. Good journalists are never off duty!

Thursday, May 20th:

Warwickshire 600 for 6 declared. Sussex 84 for 0.

On a very good, if slow, batting track, a first-day score of 357 for 6 appeared no more than okay but the shape of the day's play had left the force very much with Warwickshire. Still, few people expected the force to carry them on so spectacularly again today.

On a track like this you have to take your chances when they arrive but Sussex squandered another one early this morning when Frost, on 19, was dropped by Ambrose off Kirtley. They paid a heavy price. When Frost is in form he times the ball beautifully and he laid hard into anything loose, of which there was an increasing amount. The bowlers began to go through the motions, a state to which they were reduced by Bell who simply made no errors and to whom Sussex supporters warmed as they became aware that they were witnessing a special talent. Bell's first-class career started with a third-ball duck (albeit on a horror track at Edgbaston) against this lot - this was payback time.

v. Sussex at Horsham

When Bell became the youngest player to hit a double-century for Warwickshire, Sussex skipper Chris Adams offered him a warm handshake and asked if it was his first 200. Told that it was, Adams responded that it will be the first of many. A nice gesture.

Bell celebrated his 200 by showing the audience another dimension to his batting. Suddenly he was all aggression, smiting Mushtaq, Robin Martin-Jenkins and Mark Davis over long-off for sixes and chipping Mushtaq into the crowd at mid-wicket. The onslaught secured Bell the highest individual score in first-class cricket at Horsham, relegating Phil Mead's 224 for Hampshire in 1921 to second-best. Frost meanwhile eased to his third first-class century and posted a career-best 135 (249 balls, 17 fours) before Knight finally called a halt at 600. Another single would have given Bell and Frost the biggest stand ever for the Bears against Sussex. As it is their 289 nestles alongside the 289 stacked up by Dougie Brown and Ashley Giles also, remarkably, for the seventh wicket, at Hove four years ago. Bell's colossal effort consisted of nine hours 42 minutes batting for an unbeaten 262 from 481 balls with 27 fours and six sixes. Who knows how long he might have continued without the declaration?

Now came the hard bit. Taking wickets. Fresh from wrecking Surrey, Pretorius and Carter charged in but Ian Ward and Richard Montgomerie were little troubled. And when they did err the Bears failed to capitalise. Ward, on 10, edged Pretorius but Knight dropped a sitter in the slips. No further vestige of opportunity was offered before a surprise post-tea downpour lopped off the last hour and a half.

The grand total of no wickets fell during 83 overs in the day and, with the pitch showing no sign whatsoever of breaking up, this contest looks doomed to a draw already. But there was the privilege of watching Bell's innings - the sixth highest in Warwickshire's history. Masterful batting in a beautiful location.

The Year of the Bear

Friday, May 21st:

Sussex 464 for 7.

8a.m. in Horsham. Sunny already. Across the stirring town, windows were flung open. Radios were turned on and breakfasts taken in the fresh, warm air. Citizens of southern England popped out for papers. Shopfronts were thrown open. Aromas of croissant and bacon sandwich began to circulate. Many dogs were walked, including a particularly ludicrously sculpted poodle making its way up Blackbridge Lane in the company of an elderly man who may or may not once have been a loss adjuster. In spacious, well-manicured gardens, washing was hung out, roses were sniffed and bird tables were refuelled and at Cricketfield Road the white lines of the creases were replenished ready to play host to another day of batting gluttony.

Giles is playing in the Test, so if the Bears were to make inroads into Sussex's batting they needed one of their secondary spinners to step forward. But the auspices in the first hour were not good as Ward and Montgomery advanced smoothly. Warwickshire-born Montgomery likes Horsham. He had scored centuries on each of his last three championship appearances here and you'd have staked good money on another one here. But if you had done that you would - as all gamblers do in the end - lose. The Bears got lucky. After the openers added 143 in 37 overs Wagh slipped in a waist-high full toss and a surprised Montgomerie ladled it to Richardson at mid-on.

When, 12 runs later, Murray Goodwin dragged another innocuous Wagh offering on to his stumps, it was 155 for 2, and members of Section 19, the Bears' deeply loyal and just as knowledgeable knot of travelling supporters, had not abandoned hope of the follow-on.

Ward was full of determination though. Past 50 he slowed down to take every care to reprise Bell's role. Anyway there was no need to hurry while Adams was at the other end batting with typical brio. The Sussex captain hoisted Hogg for successive sixes over the ice-cream van at long-on in a calculated assault which further polarised the Australian's start for the Bears. He's been brilliant with the bat but the fact that he came on to bowl here after Wagh and Troughton illustrated Knight's lack of confidence in him. Hogg's frustration peaked when umpire Barrie Leadbeater rejected a particularly quixotic lbw shout. Long and loud did the spinner chunter on and he was lucky that Leadbeater, one of the best-natured of umpires, is also one of the most tolerant. Hogg would do well to recall the 1755 *Code of Laws of Cricket* which clearly stated: "Each umpire is ye sole judge of all nips and catches, ins and outs, good or bad runs and his determination shall be absolute. They are sole judges of all hindrances, crossing ye players in running and standing unfair to strike and in case of hindrance may order a notch to be scored." That message is 249 years old but still pretty valid.

Ward and Adams, assisted by more fallibility from Knight and Wagh in the slip cordon, added 194 to take their side substantially towards the follow-on figure of 451 and the match to the brink of death. There was a post-tea wrinkle when, for the second match running, Pretorius and Carter seized the second new ball and troubled two accomplished and well-set batsmen. Pretorius, assisted by one that kept low, ended Ward's stay at one minute short of six hours. The South African then had Ambrose caught in the cordon and beat Martin-Jenkins for pace first ball. Carter, meanwhile, beat the bat and hurried even the well-set Adams but without reward.

Adams lodged a muscular 144, from only 183 balls with 17 fours and four sixes, and steered his team to within sight of the follow-on figure before edging Richardson to Frost. The sun was completing its well-practised arc and those Horsham gardens were starting to fill with refugees from Crawley offices chilling out and thirsting for the latest golden prose from Bruce Talbot in the *Brighton Evening Argus*, when Matt Prior fell lbw offering no shot to Brown to bring the flurry of wickets to an end. Mark Davis and Mushtaq Ahmed fiddled their way into the 20s before the close and, despite the worthy fightback by the Bears' seamers, with just a day left and the match not yet into its third innings there are, as they say, two chances of this match generating a decisive result: Slim and None. And Slim's just headed off up the A24 in the direction of Holly Gate Cactus Garden.

The Year of the Bear

Saturday, May 22nd:

Sussex 562. Warwickshire 188 for 2.

**MATCH DRAWN.
SUSSEX 11 POINTS, WARWICKSHIRE 11.**

*"It is this deep blankness is the real thing strange.
The more things happen to you the more you can't
Tell or remember even what they were.*

*The contradictions cover such a range.
The talk would talk and go so far aslant.
You don't want madhouse and the whole thing there."*

The words of the late William Empson sprang to mind today. Why? Well, if the final day of the Bears' tussle with Surrey last week was truly memorable and featured everything that is good about championship cricket - a fluctuating plot, high levels of skill and endeavour, rising tension, joyful unpredictability and a compelling build-up to a brilliant climax - the final day at Cricketfield Road was the absolute opposite. It was, well, nothing really. A quantity of white figures moving around a field without much design or any vestige of end-product. Like cattle grazing.

County championship cricket can never be a non-stop extravaganza of thrills and spills. Of hour after hour, day after day of heroic deeds, cut-and-thrust action and sustained excitement, it simply cannot consist. It's not built that way. And anyone seriously expecting a perpetual thrillfest where every over brings a new raft of fireworks, mayhem and vicissitudes is quite simply being unreasonable. Any contest lasting four days just can't deliver that.

But the county championship does, on occasions, appear to hold its audience in baffling contempt. At a time when the bold new world of Twenty20 is spearheading the laudable drive to attract new punters into grounds, it still appears acceptable enough at times to serve up any old nonsense to some of the existing customers. At Horsham today they were asked to witness utter futility. It was awful.

v. Sussex at Horsham

A decent last-day crowd turned up this morning but many had cleared off by lunchtime to watch the FA Cup final. By then the cricket had long since disappeared in ever-decreasing circles into painful oblivion.

The captains having decided to allow the match to peter out, Sussex's tail batted through the morning with only one moment of discomfort; a Richardson yorker which seared into Mushtaq's big-toe to trigger an lbw decision and heavy bruising. The home side inched colourlessly to within 38 of Warwickshire's score. Meanwhile, one by one, the spectators drifted off to the merciful respite of sleep, the bar facility, reminiscences of Roly Thompson's hat-trick here for the Bears in 1956 (when he whipped out a trio of specialist batters Don Smith, Jim Parks, Dennis Foreman) or the exit.

The futility of it all ("Was it for this the clay grew tall? O what made fatuous sunbeams toil to break earth's sleep at all?" - was Wilfred Owen really reflecting on the savagery of war?) only increased when the Bears went in again. With Mushtaq off the field nursing his tootsie and the pitch resolutely refusing to disintegrate, motions were gone through. The only conviction in evidence came from the Horsham CC officials resolutely defending a pitch on which, without declarations, 10 days would probably be pushing it for a result.

Knight accrued the 60th first-class half-century - and one of the cheapest - of his career. Bell resumed where he left off on Thursday to compile an unbeaten 62. When the end finally came Bell had been on the field for all but 90 minutes of this match and batted for 725 minutes without being dismissed. He'd probably like to take this pitch round with him, but if he did there would be a mass suicide by the Bears bowlers.

RIP this game. At least Warwickshire took a beefy haul of bonus points and, unbeaten after four games, sit fourth in the First Division table on 48 points behind leaders Kent (59), Lancashire (55) and Middlesex (54).

****

The Year of the Bear

SCORECARD

Warwickshire 1st innings

*NV Knight		b Akram	26
MA Wagh	c Ambrose	b Akram	20
IR Bell	not out		262
IJL Trott	lbw	b Mushtaq Ahmed	26
JO Troughton		b Mushtaq Ahmed	10
DR Brown	c Prior	b Mushtaq Ahmed	21
GB Hogg	c Adams	b Mushtaq Ahmed	68
+T Frost	not out		135
Extras	(b 1, lb 5, w 1, nb 20, pen 5)		32
		Total	**600**
			for 6 dec

A Richardson, NM Carter and D Pretorius did not bat.

FoW: 1-49, 2-62, 3-108, 4-140, 5-166, 6-311.

Akram 29-2-94-2, Kirtley 28-3-130-0, Martin-Jenkins 23.4-6-62-0, Mushtaq Ahmed 50-6-194-4, Davis 31-3-96-0, Adams 4-1-13-0.

Sussex 1st innings

IJ Ward		b Pretorius	160
RR Montgomerie	c Richardson	b Wagh	61
MW Goodwin		b Wagh	9
*CJ Adams	c Frost	b Richardson	144
+TR Ambrose	c Knight	b Pretorius	1
RSC Martin-Jenkins		b Pretorius	0
MJ Prior	lbw	b Brown	17
MJG Davis	c Frost	b Pretorius	39
Mushtaq Ahmed	lbw	b Richardson	62
M Akram		b Brown	34
RJ Kirtley	not out		8
Extras	(b 9, lb 8, nb 10)		27
		Total	**562**
			all out

FoW: 1-143, 2-155, 3-349, 4-383, 5-383, 6-402, 7-418, 8-498, 9-523, 10-562.

58

v. Sussex at Horsham

Pretorius 33-7-119-4, Carter 29-6-104-0, Hogg 17-4-68-0, Brown 29.3-5-74-2, Richardson 25-7-82-2, Wagh 18-4-81-2, Troughton 6-0-17-0.

Warwickshire 2nd innings

*NV Knight	c Kirtley	b Davis	59
MA Wagh	lbw	b Kirtley	14
IR Bell	not out		6
IJL Trott	not out		40
Extras	(b 7, nb 6)		13
		Total	**188**
			for 2

JO Troughton, DR Brown, GB Hogg, A Richardson, +T Frost, NM Carter and D Pretorius did not bat.

FoW: 1-57, 2-91.

Akram 6-1-33-0, Kirtley 10-4-23-1, Martin-Jenkins 10-2-36-0, Davis 19-1-68-1, Adams 5-1-12-0, Montgomerie 4-0-9-0.

Umpires: B Leadbeater and P Willey.

****

Warwickshire missed the intervening round of totesport League games, so three days later went straight into their third successive championship match without one-day distractions. Brad Hogg had travelled to Zimbabwe for a short tour with Australia's one-day squad so Michael Powell, full of runs in the 2nd XI, was called in. That was due to be the only change. But then. . .

****

Five

v Worcestershire
at Edgbaston

Tuesday, May 25th:

Worcestershire 373 for 8.

Naqaash Tahir started this day expecting it to be just a regular sort of day. He figured on doing the sort of things that an up-and-coming cricketer normally does. In his case, today, open the bowling for Warwickshire 2nds against Nottinghamshire in the leafy environs of Knowle & Dorridge CC.

Ha. What did he know?

Until approximately 10.30a.m, Tahir's day duly continued along those predictable lines. The 20-year-old seam bowler was there warming up at Station Road ready to assail the Nottinghamshire batsmen. Then his day took a twist. A frantic message arrived from headquarters to the tune of 'Get your ass over 'ere pronto'. And half an hour later after a headlong rush across Birmingham and the briefest pause to dump his gear in the dressing room, Tahir was out on the field at Edgbaston making his championship debut.

The sudden vacancy arose when Pretorius reported an overnight back twinge. And it was fortunate for Warwickshire that the 2nds were not only at home but also playing at a venue so close, because the bowlers were straight into action after Knight's 100 per cent record with the toss was cruelly shattered. Worcestershire skipper Ben Smith called correctly and elected to bat. Tahir's time was near.

v. Worcestershire at Edgbaston

With Pretorius absent, Brown shared the new ball with Carter and it was soon evident that the pitch was far removed from the bowlers' purgatory of Horsham. Several deliveries scuttled through to Frost while others climbed. One steepled away over the wicket-keeper for byes to trigger memories of Curtley Ambrose's famous missile to Michael Atherton in the 1995 Test here. The pitch was capricious from the off. So with that in mind Knight was justifiably aggrieved to see Worcestershire pass 200 not long after lunch with only two men out.

Stephen Moore went early, caught by Trott in the gully from a booming inside-edge off his pad, but against largely ill-directed bowling Stephen Peters and Graeme Hick added 76. Knight's planning, already affected by the loss of Pretorius, was further damaged by the struggles of Richardson. Put on early in the hope that he would do what he does best and secure an end for ages *à la* Johnny Shilton, Syd Santall, Tom Cartwright or Tim Munton, unfortunately Richardson's rhythm was all awry. It was more Santa than Santall as his first three balls were woefully short and powered away for four by Hick. Knight was forced to turn to Bell for the 13th over of the innings.

At the City End, meanwhile, Tahir's moment arrived. Instead of the fledglings of Nottinghamshire 2nds, he found himself running in to bowl to the run-monster that is Graeme Hick. . . and he responded impressively. With no trace of nerves, Tahir showed the control his colleagues lacked. He was right on the spot and any bowler that lands plenty on the spot on this strip will enjoy success. Sure enough a good-length ball exploded off a length and Peters edged to Frost to supply Tahir - Birmingham-born and a product of the Bears' youth system - with his first championship wicket. Smiles all round.

They were the last from Warwickshire for quite a while. Hick was circumspect when the ball was straight but brutal on anything wide. He raced along while Smith began at a crawl (three runs from 67 balls) but grew in momentum to collect 12 fours on his way to 67. When the captain edged Brown the third-wicket had yielded 141 and on a dodgy surface, Worcestershire were heading for a position of considerable strength at 223 for 3.

The Year of the Bear

With Hick in control, the Bears had to keep nipping out his partners. The big-hearted Richardson struck back when Vikram Solanki fell to a misjudged pull. Bell earned deserved reward for a long, accurate spell from the Pavilion End when Gareth Batty nicked behind. But Hick was immense. Here was one in the eye for those critics who think he is no more than a flat track bully. A flat track this certainly ain't but he towered over the day with a mighty 158 from 263 balls with 24 fours and a six. He looked sure to remain unbeaten overnight only to be run out by Carter's direct hit - it was the only way Warwickshire were going to get him.

Buoyed by that late fillip the Bears fought hard in the last hour to retrieve a poor day's work. They ousted Bichel and Rhodes, the latter supplying Tahir with his second wicket, but 373 for 8 is a commanding effort on a pitch that umpires John Hampshire and Roy Palmer have reported to Lord's.

Wednesday, May 26th:

Worcestershire 379, Warwickshire 405.
Worcestershire 70 for 2.

ECB pitch liaison officer David Hughes was duly dispatched to observe the second day. Lucky fella.

Now this might appear a grandiose and ludicrous claim but here goes. This must rank among the most entertaining day's cricket in the history of the sport anywhere in the world. It yielded 481 runs, 14 wickets, breathtaking hitting, flying stumps, fine catches, more than a dozen leg-byes and a wildly swinging balance of power. "It's wild, its wacky - it's Warwickshire v Worcestershire in the county championship." If that's not a slogan waiting for somebody to make a fortune out of it, I don't know what is.

First up, Tahir produced two good straight 'uns to tidy up the remnants of Worcestershire's first innings. The youngster's first champo analysis stands at 17-1-47-4, an excellent start, knocking into a cocked hat the debut figures of many an illustrious bowler. The great Eric Hollies for example (27-1-150-1 for the Bears against Sussex at Edgbaston in 1932). Or Bob Willis (13-0-65-0 for Warwickshire against Worcestershire at Edgbaston in 1972).

v. Worcestershire at Edgbaston

Or Steve Harmison (9-1-77-0 for Durham against Leicestershire at Chester-le-Street in 1996). They would have given their right arms for a 17-1-47-4.

From the heights of 223 for 2 and 357 for 5, a total of 379 was a disappointment for the visitors but then the Bears' top-order again got itself in a pickle. Andy Bichel and Matt Mason, pitching the ball up intelligently, took two wickets apiece to reduce Warwickshire to 50 for 4, still worryingly remote from the follow-on figure of 230.

Troughton and Powell, new at the crease together, conferred and reached a conclusion. There was little point in passive defence on this strip because sooner or later you'd get one that was unplayable. So anything vaguely resembling a run-scoring opportunity, they went for. The result was a vivid counter-attack with Troughton driving gloriously and Powell middling as much as anyone could expect to middle on such an untrustworthy track. The home supporters rallied behind a gutsy response as the fifth-wicket pair saw off the tiring Bichel and Mason and took toll of much weaker back-up bowling by Mark Harrity and Nadeem Malik. They added 124 before Bichel and Mason returned to strike again in successive overs. Troughton fell for 67 from 73 balls and Powell for 49 from 81 and, despite their defiance, the double blow passed the initiative straight back to Worcestershire. At 174 for 6, the Bears' last four wickets still needed to find 56 to avert that follow-on.

Brown and Frost, just as Troughton and Powell had, started out fresh at the crease together and, just like their predecessors there, they attacked. Brown went for broke with such conviction that even when he top-edged the ball invariably carried clear. Bichel was clubbed for 27 in two overs. Frost was brimming with confidence from his career-best at Horsham and as Brown knocked both the ball and the bowling out of shape they thrashed 97 in 58 minutes before Frost was castled by Bichel.

Worcestershire were creaking. Heads were dropping. Enter Carter. And the beefy left-hander managed to achieve what appeared impossible - he upped the run-rate.

Carter and Brown matched each other stroke for stroke in a scintillating assault on the bowling which, rather than rising to the challenge, crumbled beneath it. Hefty hooks, lacerating drives, withering cuts, outrageous edges - they were all there, rapturously received by an incredulous crowd. This made Twenty20 appear Mogodon itself. Not much stretches the nimble fingers and agile brain of David Wainwright but on this occasion, there in his lair beside the electric scoreboard, smoke was detected coming from the Wainwright pencil and steam from the Wainwright lug 'oles.

Brown finally holed out for a wonderful run-a-ball 82 including 10 fours and four sixes. Tahir casually strolled into the carnage and joined in with a boundary or two, but the defining moment of a staggering afternoon arrived when Carter moved Warwickshire in front by nonchalantly mowing Bichel over point for six. The ball landed among the cheering Bears members as the bowler stood, hands on hips, thinking dark thoughts.

Carter was last man out when, attempting to reach three figures in the grand manner, he perished for 95. The tenth wicket had added 35 in 28 balls, of which Richardson's share was a stylish 20-minute unbeaten 0. Carter hit six sixes and nine fours in a stay of 80 balls and having recently helped orchestrate Surrey's downfall with the ball, had now executed Worcestershire's with the bat. As the standing ovation for his innings died down, it gave way to a rush of excited chatter - always a sign that something special has occurred.

Remarkably, from the wreckage of 50 for 4, the Bears led by 26. But never mind the extent of the recovery, what about the manner of it? Their total of 405 included 59 fours and 10 sixes. 44 overs between lunch and tea yielded 245 runs. Numbers five to ten had between them scored 336 from 362 balls. That's batting depth.

The cricket could only be sedate by comparison when Worcestershire went in again but still one big twist remained in the day. After Peters offered no shot to a Brown delivery that knocked out off-stump, Moore and Hick negotiated their way through until bad light closed in at 6.30p.m. Job done. . . or maybe not. Just as this mesmerising day appeared over, out came the sun again as if reluctant to let go. At 6.56p.m. out went the players for six more overs - and in the third of them Hick, having moved with customary authority to 29 from 34 balls,

John Inverarity looks forward to the new season.

Above: Out of the shadows
- the squad pose for pre-season photographs.

Below: Nick Knight leads The Bears out for the opening
game of the season against Middlesex at Edgbaston.

**Dewald Pretorius launched the glory season
in rock-solid fashion - with a dot ball.**

Nick Knight and Mark Wagh venture out
for The Bears' first innings of the season.

Above: Trott reaches 50 against Middlesex...
Below: ...as the Thwaite scoreboard dutifully records
the game's death throes on the final day.

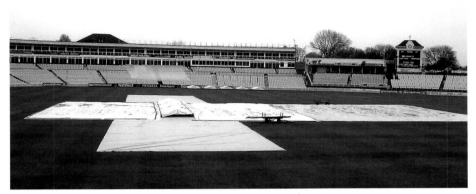

Above: Covers on for the first two days
of the home game with Gloucestershire.

Below: At last, on the third morning,
Pretorius opens up, but The Bears' season
starts with two rain-ruined draws.

Dougie Brown's 400th wicket for The Bears lifted him
alongside Freddie Calthorpe, Tom Cartwright, Frank
Foster, Billy Ibadulla, Billy Quaife, Sydney Santall
and Bob Wyatt as harvesters of 400 wickets
and 6,000 runs for Warwickshire.

Above and below: Brad Hogg reaches and celebrates his century, taking the initiative for The Bears in the first innings of the game against Surrey.

Ashley Giles's England duties allowed him just one championship game, at home to Surrey, but he played a major role with bat and ball as Warwickshire kick-started their season with a remarkable victory.

Above: As Surrey try to save the game at Edgbaston, Pretorius bowls to a watchful Butcher who, left, leaves the field at the end of the third day unbeaten on 114.
Butcher went on to reach 184, but Pretorius had the last laugh when he bowled the left-hander early on the final afternoon to trigger a stunning victory.

Knight and pinch-hitter Carter laid the foundation for a successful run-chase on the final afternoon against Surrey. Warwickshire's season was up and running.

Brad Hogg faces Sussex's Mushtaq Ahmed in the
elegant environs of Horsham's Cricketfield Road ground.

Above: Knight agonisingly loses his leg bail
to miss out on the Horsham runfest.

Below: No joy this time for the ever-voluble Mushy.

Worcestershire's Graeme Hick, so often a thorn
in Warwickshire's side, built another superb
century at Edgbaston.

But Naqaash Tahir, right, a last minute call-up from the second team, followed up his four first innings wickets with four more in the second to set up The Bears' nine-wicket victory.

Ian Bell, below, added some bowling boots to his batting ones, finishing off Worcestershire with 3 for 12 and following up with an incredible 4 for 4 in the innings defeat of Middlesex at Lord's in the next game.

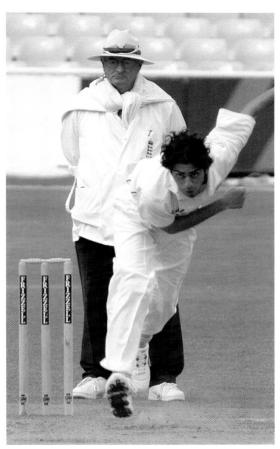

Nick Knight in solid defence: a sight which depressed
bowlers up and down the country as the captain
struck golden form in June.

got a horrible grubber from Tahir. Golden Arm accepted the lbw decision with the biggest smile this side of Holly Gate Cactus Garden and a barmy day closed with Worcestershire 44 ahead with eight wickets remaining.

And the pitch liaison officer? He's decided to come back tomorrow for another look. Who can blame him?

Thursday, May 27th:

Worcestershire 185. Warwickshire 161 for 1.

WARWICKSHIRE WON BY 9 WICKETS. WARWICKSHIRE 22 POINTS, WORCESTERSHIRE 7.

Bright and early this morning David Hughes was up there on his perch at the Pavilion End gazing out at the grass across which, playing for Lancashire in 1973, he trudged disconsolately one September afternoon having just become Lance Gibbs' 338th and last victim for Warwickshire. Three decades on he made his first note of today, probably underlined in red, after the third ball. Tahir sent one up on a good length and watched it rear to take Moore's outside-edge. 70 for 3.

This match had thrown up most things already but tossed into the pot next was a moment of fielding brilliance. Solanki was looking dangerous after swinging Tahir for a couple of leg-side sixes when he aimed another big shot, this time straight. He got underneath it and Bell, sprinting back from mid-off, kept his eye on the ball over his left shoulder, dived to get both hands round it and somehow clung on when his elbows thumped the ground. A memorable piece of work. If Tahir bowls all his career with this accuracy on this sort of pitch backed by that sort of fielding he will finish with about three million wickets.

The debutant has helped himself, of course, by putting the ball in the right place. Batty found that out to his cost, pinned lbw ninth ball. As if shell-shocked from the ordeal of the previous day, Worcestershire's middle and lower order jacked it in so spinelessly that they were all out before lunch. Smith stuck it out for 86 minutes but after he was deceived by a Carter in-ducker, the rest folded. The last four wickets, which managed only 22 runs in the first innings, contributed 29 in the second. Bell, warming up for the visit to Lord's next week, completed a great personal session by following his wonder catch with three wickets, all the product of straight, full-length bowling.

The collapse left Warwickshire facing a target of 160 in two sessions and one over. How straightforward would that be on a pitch on which 30 wickets had fallen in just over two days? Not straightforward at all, was the thinking, if Bichel and Mason bowled like they did in the first session of the match.

The Bears had one over to face before lunch and a wicket in it would have lifted the visitors again. Instead, Warwickshire lunched at 12 for 0. Knight struck Bichel for three fours and very quickly after the interval it became clear that Worcestershire's spirit was broken. Knight and Wagh added 152 at a steady four per over as the Bears cruised home. Suddenly the pitch, if not quite behaving itself, cut out the majority of its most outrageous pranks. The occasional ball grubbed but Knight batted with the assurance of a man approaching top form before copping a shooter to depart for 83 from 124 balls with 13 fours. Wagh (63 from 108 balls with six fours and a six) saw the job through and a full-house 22-point haul was banked well inside three days. Rarely have Warwickshire strung together two successive home performances of such power.

There was still unfinished business. Straight after play, groundsman Steve Rouse and the coaches and captains of both teams scampered upstairs to be quizzed by a pitch panel convened by Hughes. "Below average" was the verdict, to the Bears' relief. An embarrassment for a Test venue but no points-deduction.

Hughes emerged, grim-faced, from the conclave to announce: "There will be no comment by anyone," with a degree of gravity you might expect from a trained negotiator juggling the fate of a school full of hostages. Lighten up! It's safe to assume, though, that the pressure that Rouse is under to produce extra pitches this season due to Edgbaston part-hosting the ICC in September was taken into account.

****

v. Worcestershire at Edgbaston

SCORECARD

Worcestershire 1st innings

SD Peters	c Frost	b Tahir	31
SC Moore	c Trott	b Brown	5
GA Hick	run out		158
*BF Smith	c Knight	b Brown	67
VS Solanki	lbw	b Richardson	12
GJ Batty	c Frost	b Bell	22
AJ Bichel	c Brown	b Bell	35
+SJ Rhodes	c Frost	b Tahir	3
MS Mason	not out		14
MN Malik	lbw	b Tahir	0
MA Harrity	lbw	b Tahir	0
Extras	(b 8, lb 6, w 10, nb 8)		32
		Total	**379**
			all out

FoW: 1-6, 2-82, 3-223, 4-248, 5-291, 6-357, 7-359, 8-373, 9-373, 10-379.

Carter 18-2-70-0, Brown 24-6-83-2, Richardson 17-2-87-1, Bell 26-4-55-2, Tahir 17-1-47-4, Wagh 2-0-10-0, Trott 2-0-13-0.

Warwickshire 1st innings

*NV Knight		b Bichel	16
MA Wagh	c Rhodes	b Mason	22
IR Bell	c Hick	b Bichel	8
IJL Trott		b Mason	3
JO Troughton	c Rhodes	b Bichel	67
MJ Powell	lbw	b Mason	49
DR Brown	c Malik	b Mason	82
+T Frost		b Bichel	27
NM Carter	c Batty	b Bichel	95
N Tahir	c Batty	b Malik	16
A Richardson	not out		0
Extras	(b 9, lb 11)		20
		Total	**405**
			all out

FoW: 1-38, 2-46, 3-46, 4-50, 5-174, 6-174, 7-271, 8-330, 9-370, 10-405.

Bichel 20.1-3-126-5, Mason 22-6-80-4, Harrity 8-2-48-0, Malik 11-0-83-1, Batty 13-3-48-0.

Worcestershire 2nd innings

SD Peters		b Brown	2
SC Moore	c Frost	b Tahir	30
GA Hick	lbw	b Tahir	29
*BF Smith	lbw	b Carter	41
VS Solanki	c Bell	b Tahir	21
GJ Batty	lbw	b Tahir	1
AJ Bichel	lbw	b Bell	28
+SJ Rhodes	c Knight	b Carter	7
MS Mason		b Bell	7
MN Malik	not out		0
MA Harrity		b Bell	0
Extras	(b 9, lb 6, nb 4		19
		Total	**185**
			all out

FoW: 1-2, 2-61, 3-70, 4-98, 5-111, 6-156, 7-178, 8-182, 9-185, 10-185.

Brown 7-0-40-1, Carter 12-1-44-2, Tahir 10-0-43-4, Richardson 9-0-31-0, Bell 7-3-12-3.

Warwickshire 2nd innings (target 160)

*NV Knight		b Moore	83
MA Wagh	not out		63
IR Bell	not out		5
Extras	(lb 2, nb 8)		10
		Total	**161**
			for 1

IJL Trott, JO Troughton, MJ Powell, DR Brown, +T Frost, NM Carter, A Richardson and N Tahir did not bat.

FoW: 1-152.

v. Worcestershire at Edgbaston

Bichel 8-0-51-0, Mason 6-2-10-0, Malik 8-1-21-0, Harrity 5-0-26-0, Batty 7-0-21-0, Moore 6.3-1-30-1.

Umpires: JH Hampshire and R Palmer.

****

Beat KENT by 9 wickets (C&G Trophy), Lost to GLAMORGAN by 13 runs (totesport).

The championship joie de vivre spilled over into the prestige one-day tournament with a surprisingly easy C&G Trophy victory over Kent at Edgbaston. Wagh's unbeaten 102 - his first one-day century - underpinned the Bears' cruise past Kent's total of 211. The totesport League remains troublesome though. After Glamorgan posted a meaty 243 for 9 at Edgbaston, Knight's excellent 111 was wantonly unsupported as a lower-order implosion peaked with Alex Wharf's hat-trick.

In terms of four-day cricket, however, spirits could not have been higher as the Bears resumed their championship trail at Lord's. Tahir had done more than enough to keep his place so Richardson was omitted for the returning Pretorius. Hogg was also back with Powell unlucky to make way.

****

Six

v Middlesex
at Lord's

Wednesday, June 2nd:

Warwickshire 348 for 1.

When Nick Knight took over the captaincy last winter his response, when asked whether he thought the burden of leadership would affect his batting form, was typically honest. "I don't know," he said.

It was a valid question bearing in mind the travails of his predecessor Michael Powell. Just weeks before Powell captained Warwickshire for the first time in 2001 he was in the Caribbean with England 'A'. His reputation as an essentially defensive but invariably productive batsman was growing and growing.

Then he started his county captaincy with a blob against Hampshire and never fully recovered. In three years at the helm he averaged 29.05 with just three centuries from 73 championship knocks. Powell paid a heavy price for having the role thrust upon him too early. He also had to operate at a time when the miasma of paranoias and plots that so often stalk any organisation run by committee was puffing up particularly thick and acrid round Edgbaston way. In particular Powell was saddled, for two of his three years in charge, with the feud between then chairman Mike Smith and coach Bob Woolmer. Conducive to a successful team it wasn't. And fun it certainly wasn't.

v. Middlesex at Lord's

Yes, the captaincy comes with baggage. So can Knight carry it? He appears better placed to do so than Powell. Knight has taken over at the age of 34, while Powell was two weeks past his 26th birthday when he registered that first duck. Also, where Powell was caught in the cross-fire of an internecine personality conflict, Knight is working under the gentle and mutually-respecting figures of chairman Neil Houghton and coach John Inverarity.

The new skipper has pledged and pledged again to find time to work on his batting amid the myriad duties of leadership. He thought he would be okay but admitted he couldn't possibly know. Well he knows now. Fresh from a totesport League century against Glamorgan, after the opening day here at Lord's, Knight is unbeaten on 179. Against a Middlesex side which has started the season well, the captain has lifted the Bears into a marvellous position from which to dictate the match.

Knight's burst into form has brought relief all round. He started the season with scores, in all cricket, of 4, 5no, 21, 47, 1, 34, 6, 22no and 23 - patchy stuff. But he's followed that with 28, 62no, 26, 59, 16, 83, 74no, 111 and now a big ton here with power to add.

Today progressed just about perfectly for Warwickshire. After Knight won the toss and took first use of a flat pitch, he and Wagh enjoyed a productive first session. Knight took advantage of some short stuff from Lance Klusener to get the score moving briskly. He reached 50 from only 57 balls with his eighth four, sweetly driven through the covers off Paul Hutchison.

Wagh meanwhile looked set for another Lord's feast. He will always have fond memories of the place after the Bears' visit of 2001 when Wagh became only the fourth batsman (after Jack Hobbs, Percy Holmes and Graham Gooch) to score a triple century at the ground. His monumental 315 occupied 10 and a half hours but although he started confidently, today his innings was truncated eight and a quarter hours shorter than on his last visit when he edged James Dalrymple to slip just before lunch. A modicum of revenge, that, for Dalrymple. While Wagh was gorging himself three years ago, the Middlesex spinner was enduring a bracing championship debut bowl with only his maiden wicket - that of Dougie Brown - to show for 30 overs of baking toil on a plum batting wicket with a frighteningly short Grand Stand side boundary.

The Year of the Bear

If Dalrymple and his colleagues thought getting rid of Wagh today was a big step forward they were badly mistaken. Bell settled in alongside Knight for two sessions of steady acquisition. Neither of the batsmen cut loose but they simply eased their team into total control. With the seamers impotent, Middlesex captain Owais Shah used four spinners before tea but his mindset was negative. There was soon a sweeper on the cover boundary.

Bell enjoyed a reprieve on 26 when he bat-padded Chris Peploe's second ball but Ben Hutton failed to cling on. Both batsmen were past their first century at Lord's by the time they next offered a chance. Knight's determination to make this a major innings was illustrated by his scoring rate: his first 50 took just 57 balls, his second 84 and his third 118. His work became much more attrition than attraction, during which time the captain's colleagues busied themselves debating whether it would be possible to drive a golf ball from their balcony high in the pavilion clear over the Media Centre at the Nursery End. Carter reckoned so - few others agreed.

As the day lengthened, Middlesex's sagging spirits showed in shoddy fielding. Peploe was again unlucky when Knight, on 106, was missed by Nantie Hayward at mid-on. Just before the close Bell, on 114, edged Hutchison into the cordon but Dalrymple dropped it. Before Bell added another run he escaped again, this time courtesy of reserve wicket-keeper Ben Scott, on for the injured David Nash. Knight and Bell, unbeaten with tons behind them, walked up those history-soaked Lord's pavilion steps at the close full of satisfaction and reflecting that, in dominoes terms, the Bears were a street and a half ahead after the first couple of hands.

Thursday, June 3rd:

Warwickshire 608 for 7 declared.
Middlesex 76 for 5.

A grey day at Lord's with the cloud thick and the ball swinging around. How evocative is that?

We all know the history and atmosphere in this corner of St John's Wood is beyond compare. But never is the sense of place quite so thrilling as when the clouds gather low, enclosing the scene

72

so that with the wonderful old pavilion and steep stands encircling the turf it seems we are not so much outdoors as enclosed, cosy in a wonderful, supremely special chamber.

Those were the conditions today and the ball boomeranged around as it has in such weather on this plot since it was laid in 1814. How easy it was to peer out from an upper tier beneath the dark, brooding North London sky and picture glorious feats past. Out there on that expanse of green beneath that canopy of grey way back in 1887 (even before Old Father Time was perched up on the pavilion) did Surrey's George Lohmann flight and swing the ball all over the place to unpick the MCC to the tune of 57-29-62-6 on England's behalf in the governing body's centenary match. When England replied to MCC's 175 with 514, young Yorkshireman John Rawlin, in his first year on the Lord's groundstaff, got to know the famous turf quite well - his figures in England's only innings: 90-39-140-3!

How easy to imagine Leicestershire medium-pacer Dick Pougher, representing the MCC here in June 1896, lolloping in to skittle Australia for 18 with the little matter of 2.4-2-0-5. Or to picture Gubby Allen hitching up his trousers discreetly as he went about removing all ten Lancashire batsmen in 25.3 overs of bowling artistry for Middlesex in the 1929 championship. Or, three years later, Warwickshire's left-armer George Paine flighting it through the gloom for 7 for 14 in the opening game of the season to send the Middlesex side he left three years earlier all out for 62.

1972: Bob Massie. Heavy atmosphere. Cloud. Swing City. Match figures of 16 for 137. 1974: Geoff Arnold and Chris Old revelling under thick Monday morning cloud to unzip India all out for 42 in only 77 minutes. 1986: England hustled to defeat by that devastating duo Chetan Sharma and Roger Binny, as India secured their first Test victory at Lord's and terminated David Gower's reign as England captain. Great swing. Great feats. Now Neil Carter's got a tiny footnote in there too.

First up the Bears resumed their innings and, with Hayward and Hutchison bowling a much better line, batting was tougher. Bell soon had his middle and off stumps plucked out by a yorker from Hayward who added the scalps of Trott, caught behind cutting, and Troughton, lbw to another fine yorker.

The Year of the Bear

Brown also went cheaply but still there was Knight. And having ploughed through the morning session for just 32 runs the captain was galvanised again by the excellent Hogg. The Australian reached the crease after four wickets fell for 34 but responded with characteristic brio. Picking the off-side gaps with precision and full of aggression towards the spinners, he hammered 71 from 75 balls with six fours and a six to turn the tide back again.

Still there was Knight. And it was now clear when the declaration would come - when, not if, the captain made it to 300. Finally, he was there and called it a day with an unbeaten 303 in 10 hours and 36 minutes, the longest innings ever played for Warwickshire. Knight faced 489 balls and hit 32 of them for four and 119 of them for one to follow Frank Foster, Brian Lara and Mark Wagh as Bears to have scored a triple-century. An innings of great beauty it wasn't - at times, particularly when Hayward was steaming in, it was pure survival. But it was an exhibition of masterful concentration and inspiring leadership.

Inspired the Bears were when Middlesex set off in pursuit of 459 even to avoid the follow-on. Most of all Carter. Straight away he curved one away from Sven Koenig who edged to Frost. Next ball Shah, defeated by lateral movement, played on. Then Ed Joyce went back when he should have been forward and his bails exploded into flight. Sublime swing bowling. When Ben Hutton sliced Pretorius to Bell at third slip Middlesex were 28 for 4 and in utter disarray.

Their plight worsened minutes before the close thanks to the alertness of Frost allied to the doziness of Dalrymple. The batsman allowed a Brown delivery to pass by and then remained outside his crease as Frost threw down the stumps. Middlesex closed on 76 for 5 - and Bell, whose opening burst at Edgbaston in May will probably fill their nightmares tonight, has not even bowled yet.

v. Middlesex at Lord's

Friday, June 4th:

Middlesex 163 and 216 for 2.

It has become clear during this match that if Warwickshire win they will occupy the exciting and unexpected location known in the trade as 'top of the table'. What a way to round off the first third of the season that would be. But there's work to do yet after Middlesex fought hard late today to claw back some ground.

The outrageous one-sidedness of the first two days continued for a seventh session after the home side, following an hour's resistance from Paul Weekes and David Nash, lost their last five wickets for eight runs in 43 balls. It was a stunning collapse and those nightmares came true. Bell was the destroyer.

When the ball is swinging, Bell's pace is ideally tailored to capitalise. He made the breakthrough when Nash, having hung on for 89 minutes, got an edge which Frost parried and Brown clutched at slip. The sixth-wicket pair had added 83 plucky runs but from 155 for 5, Middlesex then collapsed to 163 all out. Bell floated up an inswinger to trap Klusener lbw first ball and was denied a hat-trick only by the narrowest margin when a similar Barry Woodesque delivery ducked inside Peploe's defence, but this time the lbw shout was turned down. No matter, Peploe soon edged behind and then Hutchison, like Klusener, was beaten all ends up first ball by Bell's booming inswinger. Hayward averted the hat-trick but did not face again as Weekes understandably tried to have a dig while he still could at the other end and thrashed Carter to Trott on the point boundary. A fourth wicket was apt reward for Carter but his 4 for 50 was usurped as the analysis of the day by Bell's nifty 4 for 4 from four overs. One more entry for the annals of Lord's swing.

Middlesex followed on 445 behind. They need to bat for more than five sessions to save the match and started off with much greater resolve than they showed first time round. Koenig and Hutton took a leaf out of the book of Knight and Bell and eschewed risk. They added 167 as, for the first time, the contest appeared even but then Warwickshire struck twice. Wagh had Koenig taken off bat and pad at silly point and Shah neatly pouched by Hogg at slip. Poor Shah, skippering the side in the absence of Andrew Strauss, has had a wretched time - scoring 0 and 3 and supervising in the field while 608 runs were conceded. He already has some dodgy history from this fixture. In the 2001 debacle, as Wagh's 315 lifted Warwickshire to 631 for 9, he bowled arguably the worst over ever delivered at Lord's (and then bagged a duck).

At least Shah was cheered a little by watching Hutton and Joyce stick at it resolutely after tea. Hutton reached his century in the final hour and with the Bears' swing combo of Carter, Bell and Tahir tamed, seamers Pretorius and Brown tight rather than terrifying and spinners Wagh, Troughton and Hogg contained, Middlesex will fancy their chances of saving this game tomorrow.

Hogg's bowling is a worry. Today he bowled nine overs for 34 runs while Wagh (18-2-44-2) was employed as the main spinner. A player who thrives on confidence, Hogg's cricket is a masterpiece of contrasts right now. Give him a bat and he's King Midas. Give him a ball and he's Collins Obuya.

Saturday, June 5th:

Middlesex 437.

WARWICKSHIRE WON
BY AN INNINGS AND 8 RUNS.
WARWICKSHIRE 22 POINTS, MIDDLESEX 1.

The Bears are top of the First Division, seven points clear of Kent and 22 clear of Surrey (who have played a game more). And today they showed some of the attributes that champions must possess. Patience. Persistence. Graft. They were also assisted by some pretty sieve-headed cricket from Middlesex but then Warwickshire did what aspiring champions must do. They took advantage.

A major obstacle was prised out early. Hutton added only 10 to his overnight 116 before Wagh deceived him to end a stay of five and a half hours that would have drawn a nod of approval from granddad Len. Hutton's demise triggered a fascinating session as the Bears probed away while Joyce and Weekes applied themselves

v. Middlesex at Lord's

diligently to the task of eating up time. It was compelling cricket in this grand old ground and what a shame that of London's population of approximately 4,050,435 (it's difficult to count them because they keep moving around) only a few hundred had fetched up to see it. All over this great, seething, fume-filled, grinding metropolis people were amusing themselves shopping, house-hunting, jellied-eel packing, pocket-picking, slab-grabbing, attending matinées and car-boot sales and gawping at ludicrously expensive tourist attractions instead of watching an enthralling cricket match at Lord's. Strange.

A nuance landed in the plot when Weekes was dropped by Frost down the leg side off Carter. Weekes had only 12 at the time and, a habitual thorn in the Bears' paw, was the last man they wanted to reprieve. Sure enough he was quick to punish any loose deliveries and, with the patient and correct Joyce, inched Middlesex towards sanctuary. When their fourth-wicket alliance stood at 96 and the total was 339 for 3 - 106 behind with seven wickets still in hand - Warwickshire were leaning harder and harder on their patience.

Sometimes in the face of prolonged resistance it's tempting to stop doing the sensible thing and instead deviate from the plan. To gamble. That can work but it usually just means the opposition are calling the shots. Knight, orchestrating from the infield rather than the close-cordon due to pain from taking a Hayward lifter on the hand, plumped for staying patient in the hope that Middlesex's patience would run out. It did.

When it comes to plugging away Douglas Brown is up there with the best of them, and it was the Scot who broke through with two big wickets. He inveigled Joyce, on 66 from 165 balls with 10 fours, to miscue to mid-on. Only a single was added before Weekes' judgment deserted him and he skied a pull and headed for the pavilion, for 62 from 109 balls also with 10 fours, before the ball landed in Knight's hands. It was not the last lapse of judgment from Middlesex's batsmen.

Next came Tahir's first wicket at headquarters, courtesy of another inappropriate pull, this time from Dalrymple, before Klusener's fatal waft across the line at Bell was not so much inappropriate as inane. The flurry of reckless strokes would no doubt have had those shoppers, house-hunters, jellied-eel packers, pocket-pickers, slab-grabbers, matinée-goers, car-boot sale enthusiasts and gawpers at ludicrously expensive tourist attractions of a Middlesex bent nodding their heads sagely and suggesting that was why they shunned the cricket.

Warwickshire didn't care about that and, raucously chivvying each other along, pressed on. With a draw still achievable for Middlesex if the tail came over all defiant, Knight maintained the pressure. Frost was now suffering and his hands were in a battered enough state to force him off the field and bring Ian Clifford on as substitute keeper. Concern grew again as Nash and Peploe knuckled down. Minutes ticked agonisingly by. Middlesex inched towards avoiding the innings defeat which would, of course, bring the 10-minute break between innings into play, thus costing the Bears potentially crucial time. Knight threw the ball to Pretorius. And the big man delivered.

It wasn't exactly ball of the century. But Nash tickled it down the leg side and Clifford made his contribution to the championship charge. Hutchison, having bagged a first-baller in the first innings, avoided a king pair but secured a pair when he exited to his 19th delivery. When Hayward perished to his 13th, Pretorius had completed the classic paceman's job of finishing off the tail and Warwickshire had secured victory in the absolute nick of time, just as they did here courtesy of Steve Perryman (11 for 150 in the match) in 1977. Nick Knight had been on the field for every minute of the match and the last vestige of doubt had been removed: he can handle the captaincy. It also appears that the Bears' position at the top of Division One was no early-season fluke. Plenty to celebrate, then, for John Inverarity this weekend - tomorrow is the 32nd anniversary of his dismissal of Dennis Amiss, clean bowled and done up like a kipper, in a tour match for the Australians against Warwickshire at Edgbaston.

****

v. Middlesex at Lord's

SCORECARD

Warwickshire 1st innings

*NV Knight	not out		303
MA Wagh	c Weekes	b Dalrymple	43
IR Bell		b Hayward	129
IJL Trott	c sub	b Hayward	3
JO Troughton	lbw	b Hayward	0
DR Brown	c Hayward	b Klusener	13
GB Hogg	c Hutchison	b Dalrymple	71
NM Carter	c Shah	b Weekes	13
+T Frost	not out		11
Extras	(b 2, lb 11, w 5, nb 4)		22
		Total	**608**
			for 7 dec

D Pretorius and N Tahir did not bat.

FoW: 1-118, 2-372, 3-382, 4-382, 5-406, 6-556, 7-579.

Hayward 26-4-82-3, Klusener 28-3-104-1, Hutchison 32-5-92-0, Hutton 12-1-45-0, Dalrymple 21.4-2-99-2, Peploe 10-2-33-0, Weekes 28-1-120-1, Shah 1-0-3-0, Joyce 4-0-17-0.

Middlesex 1st innings

BL Hutton	c Bell	b Pretorius	17
SG Koenig	c Frost	b Carter	1
*OA Shah		b Carter	0
EC Joyce		b Carter	5
PN Weekes	c Trott	b Carter	70
JWM Dalrymple	st Frost	b Brown	19
+DC Nash	c Brown	b Bell	29
L Klusener	lbw	b Bell	0
CT Peploe	c Frost	b Bell	3
PM Hutchison		b Bell	0
M Hayward	not out		0
Extras	(b 9, lb 9, w 1)		19
		Total	**163**
			all out

FoW: 1-12, 2-12, 3-22, 4-28, 5-72, 6-155, 7-155, 8-163, 9-163, 10-163.

Pretorius 11-2-29-1, Carter 16.3-2-50-4, Brown 11-3-33-1, Tahir 9-1-29-0, Bell 4-1-4-4.

Middlesex 2nd innings (following on)

SG Koenig	c Brown	b Wagh	57
BL Hutton	lbw	b Wagh	126
*OA Shah	c Hogg	b Wagh	3
EC Joyce	c sub	b Brown	66
PN Weekes	c Knight	b Brown	62
JWM Dalrymple	c Hogg	b Tahir	17
+DC Nash	c sub	b Pretorius	32
L Klusener	lbw	b Bell	12
CT Peploe	not out		19
PM Hutchison	c sub	b Pretorius	0
M Hayward	c Carter	b Pretorius	7
Extras	(b 14, lb 21, w 1)		36
		Total	**437**
			all out

FoW: 1-167, 2-173, 3-243, 4-339, 5-340, 6-362, 7-393, 8-411, 9-421, 10-437.

Pretorius 27.3-6-86-3, Carter 29-9-64-0, Tahir 12-3-38-1, Brown 18-4-46-2, Wagh 30-2-85-3, Bell 8-3-14-1, Troughton 6-1-16-0, Hogg 23-0-53-0.

Umpires: B Dudleston and TE Jesty.

****

v. Middlesex at Lord's

Lost to HAMPSHIRE by 28 runs (totesport).

From London the Bears went straight down (literally, hitting the road an hour after play and seven successive sessions in the field) to Southampton where their totesport League tribulations continued. Hampshire (fresh from two days rest having lost their championship match inside two days) amassed 241 for 5 in reply to which the Bears were always off the pace. No-one reached 40 as the innings petered out for 213.

Three days later, back in the championship, Northamptonshire visited Edgbaston. Favourites for relegation, the maroon-capped ones arrived placed one from bottom in the First Division and still to record a win after seven games. If Warwickshire could lodge the expected victory they would be in a position of real command in the championship race. They were boosted by the long-awaited arrival of Zimbabwean all-rounder Heath Streak. He came in for his debut while Pretorius dropped out.

****

Seven

v Northamptonshire
at Edgbaston

Wednesday, June 9th:

Northamptonshire 329, Warwickshire 13 for 0.

Missing a train can be a source of considerable angst and inconvenience. Missed trains have, over the years, led to all manner of terrible consequences from broken engagements and lost jobs to missed kick-offs and stranded weasels. Generally they are bad news.

But when, way back in the winter of 1914, the Reverend Archibald Hugh Conway Fargus missed his train it turned out to be very good news indeed. The clergyman subsequently had every reason to offer heartfelt thanks to the God in whose service he so diligently worked, for failing to get that choo-choo.

Following his ordination by the Bishop of Winchester in 1906, Fargus became a chaplain in the Royal Navy. Between 1907 and 1913 he served on numerous craft: HMS Encounter, Jupiter, Prince George, Zealandia and Prince of Wales. They were relatively serene peacetime postings but when the First World War broke out Fargus was destined for active service. Appointed acting chaplain to HMS Monmouth, a 9,800-tonne armoured cruiser under Admiral Sir Christopher Cradock, he was due to join it for departure for duty in the Pacific late in 1914. And that's where the missed train came in - or rather went out, without him.

v. Northamptonshire at Edgbaston

Fargus missed his connection and the Monmouth sailed without its man of the cloth. He was appointed to another ship. And it was aboard that vessel that the quietly-spoken westcountryman no doubt felt a shiver go down his spine when news arrived that on November 1st, 1914, the Monmouth, pitched into a hopeless battle with a far superior German fleet off the coast of Chile, had gone down with all hands. A narrow escape. Just as well for Fargus that he missed that train.

Now you might be wondering what in the wide, wide world of sports all that has to do with Warwickshire's 75th home championship fixture with Northamptonshire at Edgbaston which began today, nine decades on? Well...more than you think. All will become clear.

Today Heath Streak at last entered the Bears' title quest. And a right ropy old start to his Warwickshire career he made too. Fresh, or rather rusty, from several months confined to meeting rooms trying to resolve the chaos of Zimbabwean cricket, he steamed in from the Pavilion End after Northamptonshire won the toss and chose to bat. His first two overs were spent trying in vain to locate the batsman's half of the pitch. As Streak kept dropping short Tim Roberts smacked the ball gratefully to the fence to leave the bowler with figures of 2-0-18-0. The members were unimpressed. From the cheap seats an anguished cry of: "Bring back Paul Dunkels" rose and hung in the air like a prowling kestrel.

But then with the first ball of Streak's third over everything changed. This missile was right on the spot and deviated sharply in the direction of Sir Harry's. Roberts nicked it, Frost tossed up the catch, Northamptonshire were 24 for 1 and Streak was underway. Five hours later he had bowled himself into the history books with figures of 21.5-4-80-7, usurping the previous best analysis by a Bears debutant - Ed Giddins' 31.2-5-89-6 against Durham at Edgbaston in 1998, the fixture which was, you will recall, Darren Altree's only championship appearance for the Bears.

After that loose start, which was understandable enough as the 30-year-old had not played first-class cricket for months, Streak settled into an immaculate line and length. After Brown chipped in with the wicket of Robert White, caught at second slip, it was the debutant who hoisted the Bears into command with a second spell of high class. Martin Van Jaarsveld, having advanced belligerently to 46, fell lbw to one that cut in sharply. Usman Afzaal batted promisingly for 56 minutes but then got a jaffer which left him to take the edge. Streak saved his best for David Sales. The Northamptonshire captain departed ruefully after playing a perfectly sound defensive shot to a ball which pitched middle and straightened to hit the top of off.

Carter joined in with a brace of tasty yorkers to rearrange the furniture of Graeme Swann and Gerard Brophy, and at 185 for 7 Sales was wondering about the wisdom of his decision to bat first. But Streak could not bowl all day and, while he rested, Ben Phillips counter-attacked. Phillips had not previously reached 50 since joining Northamptonshire in 2002 but now did so in a hurry, using his long stride and uninhibited swing of the bat to loft the ball to good effect. Against such aggression the seamers were impotent and the spinners made no impression. While Johann Louw held up an end, Phillips thundered to 90 from 114 balls with 17 fours and two sixes as the eighth-wicket yielded 122 in 36 overs. The Bears' excellent early work was unravelling. Then Streak came back.

Armed with the second new ball his fourth delivery powered into Louw who was trapped lbw halfway through a crooked defensive shot. Phillips then perished in a cavalier fashion appropriate to his innings. He connected well with a hook but it proved one lofted shot too many as Carter took a fine catch at long leg. When Stefan Jones played back to a ball that, the way it turned out, he could not have been any worse off attempting to reverse-sweep, Streak had finished the job with 7 for 80. He left the field to loud applause - a feat hitherto exclusively reserved this season for the batsmen - and appears every inch the spearhead for which Warwickshire have been hoping.

Knight and Wagh faced five overs before the close and, as befits an opening pair fresh from adding 152 against Worcestershire and 118 against Middlesex, were little troubled. Another groovy day at the office.

v. Northamptonshire at Edgbaston

Thursday, June 10th:

Warwickshire 334 for 5.

Ah, June 10th. A day which, as far back as cricket has been played, has arrived in the second week of June. Summer starting to deepen, the year nearing its longest day, outfields quickening, Wimbledon approaching, sandwiches stiffening and pitches hardening. A good old-fashioned true cricketing day. On June 10th, spectators arrive early and leave late, the air still warm as the sun sets on a day of exploits to reside forever in memories of thrilling cricket.

On June 10th Warwickshire's supporters traditionally witness glorious endeavours from master craftsmen. 1896: Knack Pallett, spinning the ball both ways to work through the Gloucestershire order (including W.G. for just six) on the final day only for Charles Townsend's imperturbable 77 to earn his side a draw. 1920: Crowther Charlesworth, leading light of the 1911 championship triumph but now succumbing to the booze (against the Australians the previous year he wandered off when rain stopped play and was found in "a condition not fit for play" when the cricket was about to resume) peeling back the years with a coruscating 80 at Bristol. 1961: the Bears' supporters down at Blackheath revel in the sight of Ray Hitchcock, back to his best, putting Kent to the sword for an unbeaten ton to pave the way for a victory wrapped up by Basil Bridge's 5 for 2. 1985: the Edgbaston regulars can only sit back and enjoy as a bowling attack headed by Gladstone Small, Stephen Wall and Dean Hoffman is blasted for 204 by Gordon Greenidge. 1999: Muttiah Muralitharan, on his debut for Lancashire, going through the Bears' batting like a dose of salts at Southport. Ah, June 10th. Memorable cricket.

Except for today. The Bears weren't thrilling at all - just quietly efficient. They have reached the halfway point of this match five runs ahead with half of their first-innings wickets left, a strong position earned by three solid sessions that yielded 321 runs in 105 overs.

Most interest came from waiting to see how high Knight and Wagh could elevate their opening stand. Wagh drove as elegantly as ever and deposited Jason Brown over long-on for six, much to the bowler's angst. The previous ball Wagh had been reprieved when he was stranded outside his ground, only for wicket-keeper Gerard Brophy to take the ball but miss with his attempt to remove the two small wooden items from their traditional position atop the three larger ones. An embarrassing air-shot.

Knight and Wagh duly stacked up their third successive century stand. They cruised past 150, reached 189 in 60 overs and looked for all the world like they were set fair to topple the 219 by Norman Kilner and Arthur Croom at Northampton in 1933 as the best opening stand for the Bears against Northamptonshire. But then Phillips intervened as impressively with the ball as he did yesterday with the bat.

Wagh, on 92 from 169 balls, was bowled by an inswinger. Knight reached his 34th century in first-class cricket and immediately tickled a leg-glance to the wicket-keeper. Always an unfortunate way to go, and it was about the only way the insatiable Knight was going to go. When he departed, for 100 from 203 balls, the captain had been on the field for 529 consecutive overs, despite being troubled by that hand injury. His stamina and powers of concentration are the stuff of legend among his team-mates.

Bell did not quite match his captain's longevity. He was castled by another big inswinger and went for two as Phillips lodged a burst of 3 for 1 in 20 balls to sentence the second half of the day to attrition. Trott looked in good nick but after he perished on the pull, Troughton and Brown settled for escorting the Bears methodically into the lead. Troughton, under pressure with Michael Powell scoring century after century in the 2nds and the Birmingham League, needed a big score. He took 16 balls to get off the mark and batted with such impressive restraint in collecting 54 in 158 minutes that it was doubly infuriating that five minutes before the close he departed to a reckless pull, which robbed him of the chance to build that big score tomorrow.

Short of runs and short of luck, Troughton might reflect ruefully that when Brown, also just before stumps, mispulled and also offered a chance, Roberts fluffed it.

v. Northamptonshire at Edgbaston

Friday, June 11th:

Warwickshire 524. Northamptonshire 178 for 4.

Northamptonshire started this season as favourites for relegation and today they lived down to that reputation. They played some shabby cricket. The Bears, on the other hand, were purposeful and persistent and are bang on course for their third successive heavy victory. There's real momentum about their work.

When Knight lost the toss on Wednesday morning he would just about have settled for a first-innings lead of 195. Yet again the depth of the Bears' batting has earned them a stranglehold on a match. The visitors closed tonight still 17 runs behind with four second-innings wickets down, so Knight's men need only to keep doing the simple things well to win from here.

This time it was Frost, supported by Streak, who churned out the lower-order runs. Northamptonshire's hopes had risen when Hogg chopped to point and Brown gloved a lifter in the first half-hour to leave the Bears only 39 ahead with seven men out. An eighth casualty should have followed when Streak, still to score, edged into the close cordon but Van Jaarsveld emulated the fallible fielding shown by several of his team-mates and put the catch down. Costly.

Frost played with confidence and panache and it was his turn next for a reprieve, the latest beneficiary of a gaffe from the unfortunate Brophy. Northamptonshire's wicket-keeper is enduring a 'mare and when Frost, on 38, danced down the wicket to Swann he was relieved, but probably not totally surprised, to hear his fellow gauntletmeister make a hash of it. The mistake was greedily punished as Frost and Streak added 140, in the process taking the Bears past 400 in the first innings for a record-equalling fifth successive match.

Streak's batting was frill-free but effective. When he lofted Phillips for his seventh boundary, to reach 50 from 108 balls, he became the first player to lodge a half-century and five-wicket haul on his Bears debut. Finally the Zimbabwean was bowled by Swann and, after Carter's run-a-ball nine and Tahir's comparatively stodgy 10-ball one, Frost was left unbeaten 15 short of his second century of the summer. The proud son of Stoke-on-Trent had batted two hours 47 minutes, faced 122 balls and hit 12 fours.

Northamptonshire, trailing by 195, needed to bat well and long but Streak took precisely four seconds to inflict damage. That was how long it took him to chug rhythmically in from the Pavilion End and whip one inside Roberts' defence. Twenty-five minutes later White drove loosely at Carter and Brown accepted the catch in the cordon. The visitors desperately required somebody to play a major innings.

Van Jaarsveld and Afzaal both set out diligently only to give it away. The South African sparkled briefly and drove with a power that had Northamptonshire supporters of a certain age recalling Dr Harold Pretty in his pomp. But Streak drew him into playing at one he should have left, and Frost accepted the catch. Afzaal squandered the base he had laid by playing on to Brown.

Sales and Swann saw it through to the close and as long as they remain Northamptonshire have a sliver of a chance of saving the game. But the pitch is showing signs of uneven bounce and, just like a week ago at Lord's, Warwickshire go into the final day with most of the hard work done.

Saturday, June 12th:

Northamptonshire 280. Warwickshire 88 for 2.

WARWICKSHIRE WON BY 8 WICKETS.
WARWICKSHIRE 22 POINTS,
NORTHAMPTONSHIRE 5.

Now, back to the Reverend Archibald Hugh Conway Fargus. Before he started travelling the seas with the Royal Navy he was a nifty fast bowler. Born in Bristol and educated at Clifton and Haileybury he went on to study at Cambridge University, where he did enough in the summer of 1900 to earn selection for his native county. It was at Lord's, no less, where the 21-year-old made his championship debut for Gloucestershire against Middlesex and, assisted by the legendary cloud cover alluded to in a previous chapter, Fargus tore through the home batsmen for match figures of 12 for 87.

v. Northamptonshire at Edgbaston

And there's the rub. In the 104 years since, those highly impressive figures remained the best by any player on his championship debut for a county. Until now. Today, Streak airbrushed Fargus out of the history books with a second-innings haul of 6 for 78 to complete match booty of 13 for 158.

Streak hurried the Bears towards victory in the hour before lunch after Sales and Swann had batted with commendable purpose. Sales displayed the quality that makes you wonder what he might have achieved in his career with all that talent, and it took a wonderful catch to remove him. Just as the bowlers were starting to toil, a colleague helped them out with the sort of fielding that inspires a bowler just as much as a dropped sitter of a catch can depress him. Sales hooked Carter and Trott raced round from long-leg and threw himself forward to scoop the ball up inches from the turf. Terrific catch. The Northamptonshire skipper's resistance was over at dead on three hours and with him went any semblance of hope for his side.

While Brown plugged away nobly, keeping an end tight with 17 overs of graft into the wind, Streak hogged the glory. After bowling Swann he hurtled the contest to a conclusion with a burst of three wickets without conceding a run in 14 balls. Louw fenced fatally then Philips and Jones were too slow on to straight 'uns. All this from the debutant and in discomfort too from a pulled stomach muscle sustained diving in the field on the first day.

With Northamptonshire nine down at lunch and victory virtually sealed, Streak remained in the pavilion after the interval. His absence highlighted how far ahead of every other bowler he has been in this match, as number 11 Jason Brown took root for more than half-an-hour alongside Brophy. The latter showed he can bat a bit but then rounded off his personal match to forget by running himself out to leave the Bears with a target of 86 in a session and a half.

Wagh fell fencing outside off-peg and Bell was bowled third-ball by one that kept low, but Knight's irrepressible form continued. He sped to 50 from 58 balls before the winning runs arrived in handsome fashion when Trott eased Jason Brown over the long-on rope for six. Another weighty win.

The Year of the Bear

Warwickshire lead the First Division with 114 points from seven games ahead of Kent (97), Gloucestershire (79), Worcestershire (75), Lancashire (73), Sussex (71), Middlesex and Surrey (70), and Northamptonshire (57). With the more fancied counties, notably Lancashire and Sussex, struggling for consistency, the Bears are privately starting to fancy their chances. In public, of course, they have not even thought about it. "We'll just keep on trying to do the things that have got us where we are," straight-batted Knight.

All the post-match attention went to Streak of course, and he dealt with consummate patience and courtesy with the gaggle of reporters gathered in search of that journalistic gold (or, depending upon your point of view, dross); quotes. The Rev Fargus is probably looking down with a degree of wistfulness but also considerable respect for a fine fellow sportsman. Or maybe he is angry and bitter. Or maybe there is, as some suggest, no after-life at all and he's not feeling anything at all. We can't know. Nor can we know the reaction of another man displaced from the record books by Streak's 13 for 158. That analysis is the best match return by any Warwickshire debutant, and the best by any Bears bowler since the 13 for 115 lodged by fast-bowler Tony Merrick against Lancashire at Edgbaston in 1987. Now what would Merrick, for some years now residing back in his native Caribbean, make of his record having been broken? Recalling the laid-back Antiguan it's probably pretty safe to assume he wouldn't give two hoots.

****

SCORECARD

Northamptonshire 1st innings

TW Roberts	c Frost	b Streak	18
RA White	c Wagh	b Brown	18
M van Jaarsveld	lbw	b Streak	46
U Afzaal	c Frost	b Streak	21
*DJG Sales		b Streak	8
GP Swann		b Carter	35
+GL Brophy		b Carter	25
J Louw	lbw	b Streak	38
BJ Phillips	c Carter	b Streak	90

v. Northamptonshire at Edgbaston

PS Jones		b Streak	18
JF Brown	not out		0
Extras	(b 2, lb 6, nb 4)		12
		Total	**329**
			all out

FoW: 1-24, 2-64, 3-105, 4-110, 5-127, 6-170, 7-185, 8-307, 9-312, 10-329.

Streak 21.5-4-80-7, Carter 20-8-60-2, Brown 15-4-46-1, Tahir 16-4-39-0, Bell 7-2-24-0, Hogg 6-1-19-0, Wagh 9-2-49-0, Troughton 2-1-4-0.

Warwickshire 1st innings

*NV Knight	c Brophy	b Phillips	100
MA Wagh		b Phillips	92
IR Bell		b Phillips	2
IJL Trott	lbw	b Swann	44
JO Troughton	c Brown	b Louw	54
DR Brown	c Brophy	b Jones	45
GB Hogg	c Swann	b Phillips	20
HH Streak		b Swann	61
+T Frost	not out		85
NM Carter	lbw	b White	9
N Tahir		c & b Swann	1
Extras	(b 3, lb 4, nb 4)		11
		Total	**524**
			all out

FoW: 1-189, 2-194, 3-197, 4-249, 5-331, 6-358, 7-368, 8-508 9-517, 10-524.

Jones 31-5-115-1, Louw 27-6-83-1, Phillips 34-7-110-4, Brown 41-9-128-0, Swann 26.3-5-69-3, White 3-0-12-1.

Northamptonshire 2nd innings

TW Roberts	lbw	b Streak	0
RA White	c Brown	b Carter	8
M van Jaarsveld	c Frost	b Streak	48
U Afzaal		b Brown	37
*DJG Sales	c Trott	b Carter	76

GP Swann		b Streak	29
+GL Brophy	run out		41
J Louw	c Frost	b Streak	10
BJ Phillips	lbw	b Streak	0
PS Jones	lbw	b Streak	0
F Brown	not out		7
Extras	(b 2, lb 11, nb 11)		24
		Total	**280**
			all out

FoW: 1-0, 2-16, 3-83, 4-126, 5-201, 6-234, 7-257, 8-259, 9-261, 10-280.

Streak 21.5-2-78-6, Carter 25.1-5-67-2, Tahir 4-0-17-0, Wagh 3-0-14-0, Bell 11-8-10-0, Brown 23.1-5-73-1, Troughton 2-0-8-0.

Warwickshire 2nd innings (target 86)

*NV Knight	not out		56
MA Wagh	c Swann	b Louw	10
IR Bell		b Louw	0
IJL Trott	not out		22
Extras			0
		Total	**88**
			for 2

JO Troughton, DR Brown, GB Hogg, T Frost, HH Streak, NM Carter and N Tahir did not bat.

FoW: 1-29, 2-35.

Louw 7-0-27-2, Jones 4-0-32-0, Phillips 5-1-14-0, Brown 1.4-0-15-0.

Umpires: IJ Gould and JF Steele.

****

v. Northamptonshire at Edgbaston

Beat LANCASHIRE by 112 runs (totesport).
Beat NORTHAMPTONSHIRE by 73 runs (C&G Trophy).

On a high in four-day cricket, Warwickshire at last translated their champo form into the shorter formats. Emphatic back-to-back home victories suggested a tilt at trophies on every front was still possible. Knight (92) and Wagh (69) lifted the Bears to an impregnable 310 for 5 - their highest score in the one-day league - against Lancashire. Three days later Northamptonshire returned to Birmingham for a C&G Trophy quarter-final and found the hosts in even more runtastic form. Carter launched the fun with 28 from a Stefan Jones over before Hogg (94), Bell (68) and Trott (65) lifted the Bears to 343 for 5. Brown then took 5 for 43 as Northamptonshire fell well short and the Bears' dressing room echoed to mighty post-match cheers when they were drawn at home to Worcestershire in the semi-final.

****

Eight

v Lancashire
at Stratford-upon-Avon

Friday, June 18th:

Warwickshire 495 for 9.

Stone the crows. For the first time since 1992, Warwickshire have ventured to an out-ground for a home game. Since they met Middlesex at Coventry precisely 12 years and one week ago, the Bears have stuck doggedly to Edgbaston as a home venue so that supporters in the south of the county (where, of course, the club first burst into existence in the middle of the 19th century) have had to travel into Birmingham to watch their team. At last the punters in Stratford, Warwick, Stoneleigh, Pillerton Priors, Pillerton Hersey and the like can just hop down the road. About bleedin' time.

It would be nice to report that the decision to bring a championship match to Stratford CC's sylvan Swan's Nest Lane ground was a gesture of goodwill to the punters round these parts. But while some people at Warwickshire, notably operations manager Keith Cook, fought hard to make it happen for that reason, there is also a big dose of expediency behind the exercise. With Edgbaston chosen as one of the three host-grounds for the lucrative ICC Champions Trophy in September, the pressure on groundsman Steve Rouse to produce sufficient pitches this season is considerable. Taking a champo game out of the equation means

v. Lancashire at Stratford-upon-Avon

one less pitch for him to prepare and also a vacant week mid-season for him to work on the square.

The challenge for Stratford, who have only once before hosted a first-class match - Warwickshire's three-day friendly with Oxford University in 1951 (this very week in a season when they went on to win the title; another omen?) - is to present a compelling case for making this an annual event. At the end of the opening day Warwickshire's batsmen are certainly not complaining. They have piled up the thick end of 500, hitting 75 fours and a six along the way.

Pitch inspector Raman Subba Row dropped in yesterday to take a precautionary peek at the pitch and was quite happy. Mark Wagh was certainly happy with it too after he amassed a glorious 167 to impress a decent crowd (in the region of 3,000) as well as possibly double that number watching nationwide live on Sky.

Wagh was assisted by the absence of most of Lancashire's front-line bowlers. The Bears' inconvenience at losing Heath Streak to a torn stomach muscle pales in comparison to the depletion of the visitors' ranks. Championship favourites at the start of the season, Lancashire have found their hopes of a first title since 1934 decimated by injury and international call-ups. Here their seam and pace attack is shorn of James Anderson, Andrew Flintoff and Sajid Mahmood on England duty and the injured Glen Chapple and Dominic Cork. With Carl Hooper and Iain Sutcliffe also unfit the visitors have fetched up at Stratford highly patched up. Over breakfast this morning they rushed through the registration of Indian international and former Little Stoke batsman Dinesh Mongia.

With so many bowlers out Lancashire skipper Warren Hogg could seriously have done with calling correctly but he didn't, and Wagh and Nick Knight were soon advancing smoothly towards their fourth successive century opening stand. Great was the pride of Stratford chairman Paul Biddlecombe and his fellow club officers as Knight and Wagh strode out to bat and Swan's Nest Lane became the tenth venue, joining Edgbaston, Mitchell's and Butler's, Coventry Bull's Head, Coventry Butts, Coventry Courtaulds, Coventry Morris, Leamington, Nuneaton Griff and Nuneaton CC, to host championship cricket for Warwickshire.

The Year of the Bear

With so many seam options unavailable Lancashire opened up with Peter Martin, pressed into action after a lengthy injury absence, and former Durham seamer John Wood, aged 33 and with a first-class bowling average to match. On a pitch that offered them little encouragement Martin looked rusty and Wood innocuous, and in the first hour they suffered.

Knight simply accepted runs when they were offered but Wagh was in punitive mood. When his feet are moving and his confidence is high there are few finer sights in cricket than the former King Edward's School pupil dispatching the crimson rambler in front of the wicket. Today was such a day. Particularly harsh on Wood, he pulled and drove mercilessly while only the tiniest aberration of length triggered a rapacious whip through mid-wicket.

Knight garnered yet another half-century then fell on the stroke of lunch to a marginal lbw decision but the first hour of the afternoon oozed classical strokeplay. Wagh was at his best, exhibiting the quickness of eye that the best batsmen need and the richness of strokes that only very good batsmen possess. Unhindered by any lateral movement from the ball, he galloped to his 18th first-class century and, with Bell finding gaps as surely as running water does, the Bears raced along at five an over.

At 295 for 1 the sky appeared the limit but then perhaps it became too easy and both batsmen chopped innocuous offerings from Stephen Crook to Stuart Law at point. Wagh's 167 occupied only 223 balls and included 30 fours. It was craftsmanship of a high standard, albeit in perfect conditions.

The stage was set for Troughton to fill his boots on his home club ground. But, perhaps intimidated by the painful memory of having his middle-stump rattled by Simon Hollyhead here, he missed out. So did Brown and, inevitably after the strokefest that had gone before, the Bears lost momentum. It was restored by Hogg. Nimble of foot and free of inhibition he sped to 50 from only 41 balls with nine fours to lift Warwickshire over 400 with plenty of time still to add before stumps.

A highly entertaining day continued to convolute as Martin returned to show his class with a three-wicket new-ball burst. Trott was bowled offering no stroke. Hogg did offer a stroke but was bowled anyway. Frost departed lbw to secure only the fourth

Heath Streak joins the Warwickshire party and makes his spectacular debut at Edgbaston against Northants.

Above: Streak is congratulated by his team-mates as he takes yet another Northamptonshire wicket.
Below: The Zimbabwean triggers another celebratory gathering after bowling Swann as victory draws near on the final day.

Above: Wagh and Knight set about their opening
stand of 189 against Northamptonshire.
Below: The scoreboard says it all - Streak
has arrived in record-breaking style.

Nick Knight's imperious form continues
as he closes in on another ton.

Knight departs for exactly 100.

Jim Troughton delivers another devilish left-arm spinner.

Tony Frost's unbeaten 85 lifted Warwickshire into total command against Northants.

Knight and Trott leave the field having steered
The Bears to their third successive victory.

Championship cricket arrives
at Stratford-upon-Avon at last.

Below, a proud moment for all at Swans Nest Lane
as the opening day gets underway.

Above and below: It was Mark Wagh's turn to score the runs in the first innings as he plundered 167 off the hapless Lancastrians as Warwickshire totalled 499.

Neil Carter does the honours for autograph
hunters at Swans Nest Lane.

Above and below: Passing the time as grey clouds
gather over Stratford-upon-Avon.

The final day at Stratford begins in brilliant sunshine, above, but the storm clouds gather again below and the game peters out into a tame draw.

More runs for Knight as the weather-lashed contest
at Stratford drifts to a draw.

Jonathan Trott scored valuable runs all summer
and his wait for a century ended at last
against Kent at Beckenham.

Michael Powell top-scored with 134 at Beckenham
and followed that up with another vital ton
against Surrey at Guildford.

Ian Bell also hit a purple patch. Narrowly deprived of a century in each innings at Guildford, he proceeded to achieve the feat in the very next match, against Lancashire at Old Trafford.

Also in the runs was Dougie Brown with centuries at Guildford and Old Trafford. Both times he helped to steer his side out of choppy waters.

v. Lancashire at Stratford-upon-Avon

blob by a Warwickshire player in first-class cricket at Stratford-upon-Avon, joining the impressive list of Norman Horner, who bagged a pair in '51, and Roly Thompson.

The clamour of runs and wickets amounted to a cracking christening for champo cricket beside the Avon, and there was still a late flourish from Carter who thraped 32 off 30 balls, including the day's only six heaved in the direction of the Butterfly Farm. The Bears closed just a similar smite short of 500 runs in a day. Great fun for the home crowd but not so much for a beleaguered, injury-ravaged, knackered Lancashire XI who were even denied the solace of a nice invigorating shower immediately after play. Their dressing room is so small that they had to stack all their kit in the showers, so had to return to the hotel to freshen up. Not that they had any room (pardon the pun) to complain. Facilities at Blackpool, after all, are a bit less than palatial too.

Saturday, June 19th:

Warwickshire 499, Lancashire 299 for 3.

A lot of people have put in a lot of work to bring this game to Stratford (not least the army of stewards who spent Thursday evening setting out seats when they could have been watching England's footballers play Switzerland in the European Championships). So they deserve better than to see a serious downturn in the weather.

Rain took out 28 overs today but more pertinently, in terms of spectator appeal, the temperature was stripped of a few degrees by an unfriendly breeze. Nowhere was this more noticeable than in the press and scorers' tent, positioned to the right of the pavilion. Moved here from its originally intended location at long-on to make room for some of Sky's twelve million tons of apparatus, the tent is at the epicentre of all the world's draughts. On such occasions is David Wainwright heroically resolute.

Warwickshire's last wicket was briskly blown away this morning when Martin yorked Tahir (the veteran seamer's last ever Bears scalp). Tahir struck 26 from 28 balls and is surely destined to bat higher in the order than 10. The late runs that he and Carter supplied last night ensured yet another daunting total for the Bears, and again the opposition set out with avoidance of the follow-on (350 in this case) the objective before they can start thinking about a lead. Warwickshire have won a lot of tosses this season it's true. But they have also capitalised on them by scoring big runs.

Mark Chilton set off at a gallop with three successive boundaries off Carter but then edged to second slip where, to the left-armer's relief, Wagh clung on. Carter has suffered badly at the erratic hands of the close-catchers this summer.

The clouds were already gathering though and at 45 for 1 in the 14th over they administered a good dousing. Mopping up took some time and while a four-day contest can usually withstand the loss of 28 overs the interruption here, allied to the benign surface, fast outfield and modest bowling attacks, shortened the already very short odds on this match ending in a draw.

After the resumption Malachy Loye shortened them further by taking responsibility in exactly the way required by his depleted team. Alex Swann's joyless stay (20 in an hour and 49 minutes) was ended by Bell and Law failed to deliver the major innings required when he tickled a catch down the leg-side after speeding to 44 from 64 balls. But Loye was untroubled. The former Northamptonshire batsman inched forward against a bowling attack which, as most bowling attacks would, floundered on the flat track. Mongia looked a class batsman as he helped Loye add 137 before the close.

Lancashire need just another 51 tomorrow to avoid that follow-on, at which point there will be as much hope of this match generating a positive result as there is of Lester Piggott backstroking across the River Avon and streaking across the ground stark naked, save for a strip of glistening Yorkshire pudding strapped to his belly.

v. Lancashire at Stratford-upon-Avon

Sunday, June 20th:

Lancashire 505 for 8.

When this match landed in the calendar - right in the heart of summer and culminating on Midsummer's Day itself - the prospects were perfect. The chances of decent weather were as good as you are ever going to get in the notoriously fickle British climate. Might get a few showers. Or a bit of concerted rain if you're really unlucky. Might not be boiling hot. Might even be chilly. But it's safe to say that nobody ever suspected that the Swan's Nest Lane outfield would be left white by a deluge from above. Must be something about Lancashire - they were, of course, Derbyshire's visitors when it famously snowed on Buxton one June day.

Mongia went early today but the relentless Loye, in alliance with Paul Horton, took Lancashire past the follow-on figure to quietly seal the match's fate. Just before lunch a small attendance was quietly monitoring the Bears' fruitless attempts to make further inroads. At least the spectators had warm sunshine in which to watch as the players heaved their long shadows round the grass with cheerful but unmistakeable resignation to the looming draw. All was gentle and serene - until a hailstorm of biblical proportions swept the ground.

Suddenly the sky gave way. Through the air flooded a deluge of stones, some as big as basketballs. They battered marquees and thundered onto the pavilion roof. They pinged off visor of helmet, windscreen of Peugeot and beak of swan. Cricketers fled. Spectators scrambled for cover. Groundstaff leapt into action. Within 10 minutes, incredibly, on June 20th for heaven's sake, the field was white. Suddenly the pavilion bar, windows steaming up like it was midwinter, took on very cosy proportions.

48 overs were lost in one of the more spectacular interruptions of the season and by the time play resumed late in the afternoon the match was as dead as a dodo. Carter had Horton caught behind cutting and Crook mispulled Tahir to mid-off before finally the admirable Loye was removed. When he missed an attempt to force Wagh, he had been at the crease for seven hours ten minutes for 184 from 324 balls with 27 fours. His vigil was chiefly responsible

99

for the Bears missing out on a bowling point as, fuelled by a lusty cameo by Hegg, Lancashire reached the 130-over mark, beyond which bonus points cannot be collected, at 500 for 7. The last act of a day of freak weather was a piece of freak cricket - a wicket for Hogg. When Hegg played across the line in the last over the Australian collected his first championship victim for five weeks and only his fourth in all.

Monday, June 21st:

Lancashire 508. Warwickshire 124 for 2.

MATCH DRAWN.
WARWICKSHIRE 11 POINTS, LANCASHIRE 12.

Warwickshire went into this week's two games against Lancashire and then Kent (starting the day after tomorrow) aiming for at least a win and a draw. But two draws, with decent bonus points, would keep the two potential challengers nice and remote in the table. So far so good.

Realistically there was never a chance of anybody winning this game on a pitch almost Horshamesque in its contempt for bowlers. Quite understandably, as an outground, first and foremost you guard against serving up a terror track (à la Worthing, 1964) which can send your aspirations to regularly host county cricket up the Swanee forever. Swan's Nest Lane perhaps erred too far the other way, but hopefully that won't count against them when the powers-that-be meet to decide whether the Bears should return.

It all ended in a bit of a damp squib. Pretorius tidied up the Lancashire tail in no time and the rest of the day was shared between Warwickshire batting out time, showers passing by and the small crowd, as John Lennon would no doubt have described it had he reported on cricket, watching the wheels. The attendances, even bearing in mind the changeable weather, have been slightly disappointing and it's fair to say the event has leaned heavily on major sponsor Chase Midland. But let's hope the Bears are back here next season and beyond.

v. Lancashire at Stratford-upon-Avon

Logistically most went well and where it didn't go quite so well, lessons can be learned. With no precedent to work with, too much temporary seating was constructed so that extra costs were incurred just to deaden the atmosphere with empty plastic seats that masked the charm of this intrinsically pleasant ground. That charm was also eroded by Sky's multitude of paraphernalia, which won't be here next time. Also next time both dressing rooms could be used by the one team with the other housed in a temporary one. And perhaps the press could be found a more ergonomically-friendly location. Like the river.

But these were inevitable and minor teething troubles of a thoroughly creditable first stab. Welcome to the championship stage, Stratford CC. May you be around the first-class scene long-term.

Eleven points leave Warwickshire a solid 28 clear at the top at the season's halfway stage. Now it's down from one outground hosting its first champo fixture to another - Beckenham - to face Kent. Anything other than defeat there and the Bears will head into a three-week break from four-day cricket superbly placed.

****

SCORECARD

Warwickshire 1st innings

*NV Knight	lbw	b Keedy	53
MA Wagh	c Law	b Crook	167
IR Bell	c Law	b Crook	49
IJL Trott		b Martin	54
JO Troughton	c Law	b Keedy	8
DR Brown	lbw	b Mongia	16
GB Hogg		b Martin	56
+T Frost	lbw	b Martin	0
NM Carter	c Swann	b Wood	32
N Tahir		b Martin	26
D Pretorius	not out		1
Extras	(b 11, lb 5, w 1, nb 20)		37
		Total	**499**
			all out

FoW: 1-14, 2-295, 3-304, 4-313, 5-356, 6-419, 7-419, 8-446, 9-478, 10-499.

Martin 18.5-2-81-4, Wood 20-2-122-1, Chilton 5-1-22-0, Crook 18-2-78-2, Mongia 17-1-82-1, Keedy 26-5-98-2.

Lancashire 1st innings

MJ Chilton	c Wagh	b Carter	13
AJ Swann	lbw	b Bell	20
MB Loye		b Wagh	184
SG Law	c Frost	b Tahir	44
D Mongia	lbw	b Bell	89
PJ Horton	c Frost	b Carter	22
SP Crook	c Knight	b Tahir	23
*+WK Hegg		b Hogg	54
J Wood	not out		13
PJ Martin		b Pretorius	2
G Keedy	c Frost	b Pretorius	0
Extras	(b 5, lb 14, w 3, nb 22)		44
		Total	**508**
			all out

FoW: 1-19, 2-93, 3-162, 4-333, 5-381, 6-409, 7-459, 8-505, 9-508, 10-508.

Pretorius 27.3-6-76-2, Carter 16-1-93-2, Tahir 20-5-47-2, Bell 18-1-66-2, Brown 9-1-34-0, Wagh 19-1-77-1, Hogg 21-2-66-1, Troughton 4-0-30-0.

Warwickshire 2nd innings

*NV Knight	not out		67
MA Wagh	c Law	b Wood	18
IR Bell	c Hegg	b Keedy	1
IJL Trott	not out		36
Extras	(nb 2)		2
		Total	**124**
			for 2

JO Troughton, DR Brown, GB Hogg, T Frost, NM Carter, N Tahir and D Pretorius did not bat.

v. Lancashire at Stratford-upon-Avon

FoW: 1-46, 2-47.

Martin 6-1-30-0, Wood 10-1-31-1, Keedy 12-1-31-1, Swann 1-0-1-0, Crook 6.1-0-31-0.

Umpires: NG Cowley and G Sharp

****

Nine

v Kent
at Beckenham

Wednesday, June 23rd: No play.

When cricketers are kept off the field by rain they hurt more on some occasions than on others. Never, never in a million years, of course, would a stout, upstanding professional cricketer actually want rain to fall. But there are occasions when precipitation provokes a feeling of less than total devastation. Today, for example, when rain wiped out the entire opening day here in Southeast London, Warwickshire's regret was containable.

Kent trail the Bears by 28 points in the First Division so all the pressure is on them to win this match. Warwickshire have, as they say, the points on the board. They would love to win here but a draw would do, especially in the light of a dramatic injury twist that occurred late last night. The problem with Knight's left hand, sustained three weeks ago at Lord's, has been shown by a scan to be a fracture. After defying advice to rest it until now the captain has finally had to accept the folly of playing on and risking long-term absence from a further blow on the affected mitt.

So the Bears are without not only main strike-bowler Streak but also their main batsman. Knight must wait for a chance to score the 76 runs he needs for 1,000 in first-class cricket this season. To lose a player in such staggering form (he averages 99.55 this season and has amassed 662 runs in his last six innings) is obviously not desirable but the good news is that his replacement is equally full of form. Michael Powell has four 2nd XI centuries and a Birmingham League double century behind him and while those runs were scored in lesser cricket you can, as they say, only deal with what's in front of you.

Powell was summoned just as he was putting the cat out late last night and arrived at the team hotel in the early hours of this morning. He's back and so is Richardson (because Pretorius has a thigh injury) so it's a reshuffled team that acting skipper Dougie Brown will wield when the contest gets underway.

There was never a chance today as rain fell steadily. With the Bears coming to the end of a hectic sequence of four-day games, the unscheduled day off won't have done them any harm. A little gentle gym-work was undertaken but the only notable display of energy was the burst of acceleration from Steve Perryman in the direction of the turf accountant's facilities when he realised they were loading for the 2.30.

Hogg, Hollyhead and 12th man Mees played Scrabble, the coach read a book, a woman with giant tattoos on her giant and wantonly exposed breasts marched, swearing madly, through the drizzle up nearby Sydenham High Street and one or two reporters bit the bullet and, in the name of duty of course, joined Warwickshire's supporters in the pavilion bar and got quietly sozzled. Rain tumbled down, the windows steamed up, at least one round was bought to belatedly celebrate the 25th anniversary, yesterday, of Dennis Amiss being dismissed by David Bairstow in a championship match, and time passed most convivially in excellent company including the most debonair bus driver in Rugby.

Thursday, June 24th:

Warwickshire 334 for 1.

First-class centuries come in all styles. You've got the cheap variety (plundered off joke bowling), the spectacular variety (laced with big hits), the tedious variety (taking so long it damages rather then enhances the team's cause), the fortunate variety (dropped eight times and including 27 overthrows) and the laudable variety (where good judges acknowledge the landmark by putting down their papers, hitching up their trousers, turning to their neighbours and exclaiming: "Well played sah").

And then you've got the real McCoy. The bee's knees. The dog's bollocks. The special type of innings which, for whatever reason, truly deserves to be rewarded with a century. Few innings fall more deservingly into this category than Michael Powell's today.

Powell has had a rough couple of years. Pretty soon after he took on the captaincy the rapport and respect between Bob Woolmer and M.J.K. Smith was evaporating, and he was caught increasingly in the crossfire. Forced to deal with far too much politics his batting understandably suffered. A player who entered the captaincy in April 2001 as a member of England's 'A' team left it in September 2003 unable to command a place in his county side. So this season the guy who essentially sacrificed three of his peak years (and probably any realistic chance of pressing on with his England aspirations) to lead his county found himself playing 2nd XI cricket.

He never complained. Powell's not that type. He just got on with it, at whatever level, and churned out runs so that when his chance came again he was ready. It arrived against Worcestershire at Edgbaston in May, and on a shocking pitch he scored a skilful 49 to help turn the game. Now another opportunity has knocked and he went the whole hog for one of the most popular centuries of this or any season.

It wasn't the most flamboyant innings but nobody cared about that. It was a bloody good one and best of all in its crucial early stages. Warwickshire won the toss and batted on a pitch that was decent for batting but had pace. With conditions encouraging the quickies, and two teams in the running for the championship, the first session was perfectly set up for a cracking contest. As Mohammad Sami and Martin Saggers starting fizzing the ball down at Powell and Mark Wagh, a projected lunchtime score of 80-odd for 2 looked like it would be a good effort. Instead the Bears were 97 for 0 and, with four sessions of the match gone, that victory Kent so badly needed looked a million miles away.

The Bears' openers played it perfectly with excellent judgment outside off-stump, as Saggers unleashed a fine spell that had the ball thundering into wicket-keeper Niall O'Brien's gloves. In bright sunlight with a blustery wind sweeping across a pleasant, if slightly plain, grassy bowl within a drop-kick of Crystal Palace FC's training-ground, battle was joined. Two batsmen Warwickshire through and through ducked and dived against two bowlers of considerable pace.

The Bears were assisted by a bizarre spell from Sami. The Pakistani, in his last match for Kent, got it into his head that bouncers were the key to success so unleashed plenty, mostly at Powell. Most passed too high to be of remote concern so the tactic amounted to a colossal waste of energy from a high-quality bowler who could have been devastating in the conditions. The whisper is Sami would poll few votes for Kent's Players' Player-of-the-Season award and after this brainless exhibition you could see why.

So Powell and Wagh steadily steered the ship through until lunch, by which time the pitch was settling down and Kent captain David Fulton had already used six bowlers. The openers then resumed with similar composure in the afternoon and were closing in on the Bears' record opening stand against Kent - surprisingly, considering the two teams have met 121 times in the championship, it's only 196 between Dominic Ostler and Roger Twose (at Edgbaston in 1994) - when Wagh perished to Ben Trott for a fine 86 from 142 balls with 12 fours.

Jonathan Trott simply took up where Wagh left off. The 23-year-old has passed 50 four times this season but is yet to reach 100 and looked determined to rectify that. Severe on anything short he was soon catching up with the implacable Powell. Trott laid into Sami whose daft day peaked with a crass over which went for 19.

But this day was Powell's. His reaction - clenched fists and huge smile - when he reached his century, from 263 balls, said it all. So did the reaction of his team-mates on the balcony and the Bears supporters up there on the grassy knoll. This was a big century. A real statement of intent. It was Steve McQueen, as Papillon, drifting out to the ocean on a bed of corn-shucks. "I'm still here you bastards".

And it was a great job done for the team too. Powell was still there on 112 from 100 overs at the close. Trott needs just three runs in the morning for the century he covets so much. And Kent can't win this game. The Bears will break off for the three-week championship hiatus on Saturday night in a mighty position in the First Division table.

The Year of the Bear

Friday, June 25th:

Warwickshire 502 for 6 declared. Kent 249 for 8.

Maybe even mightier than they could have dreamed. There's just a chance - a tiny chance because Kent surely can't bat so carelessly second time around and the weather forecast is bad - that the Bears could win here after another day of cool-headed, strong-minded and skilful cricket peaking with an iconic flipper.

First, the Bears batted on and Trott wasted no time in reaching that precious ton, flicking Saggers to the mid-wicket fence in the second over of the day. Under orders to get on with it, the South African then edged an attempted cut. Bell was soon batting fluently, which was just as well because Powell became almost becalmed before finally lifting Ben Trott to long-leg. He had batted exactly seven and a half hours for 134 from 372 balls and it's fair to say his job was done. And his point made.

Powell's century has seriously increased the pressure on Troughton, whose place must be vulnerable when Knight is fit again. But the left-hander batted totally selflessly for a bright 21 and Hogg and Brown thrashed 49 in 20 minutes after lunch to hoist the score past 500 and trigger the declaration. The total of 502 for 6 is the Bears' highest on Kent soil, surpassing the 470 for 8, fuelled by centuries by Alvin Kallicharran and Dennis Amiss and a half-century of extras, at Folkestone in 1983. It also harvested the Bears' seventh successive haul of maximum batting points while Kent were restricted to just a single bowling point.

Still, with rain around in the south (according to reports, Holly Gate Cactus Garden is particularly vulnerable to a good dousing) it was long odds on anything but a draw until Kent's top-order imploded. Michael Carberry played round a full-length ball from Carter before Tahir, not for the first time, showed a handy knack of knocking over a wicket straight away. Replacing Brown, he bowled Ed Smith through a loose drive in his first over then had Fulton pouched by Powell in the slips. 50 for 3. Game on.

Andrew Symonds and Matt Walker added 36 before Kent found out that every Hogg has his day. Brad Hogg went into this match with four championship wickets for 479 but he responded to Brown's show of faith in him (it's doubtful whether Knight would have bought the Aussie on for the 31st over) with three wickets for 29 runs in 12 overs. In his first over he bowled Walker all ends up with that iconic flipper. Alex Loudon, surprised by bounce, bat-padded to short-leg. O'Brien, frozen like a rabbit in headlights, offered no shot to a straight one. That made it 146 for 6 with Kent still 207 short of the follow-on figure.

Birmingham-born Symonds was still there though. Blending brutality and finesse, he socked Brown over long-on for six, late-cut Bell exquisitely just wide of slip and clouted Tahir for three successive fours. Symonds posted 100 from only 108 balls and, in alliance with the stubborn Min Patel, bought Kent valuable time. Hogg beat Patel with a quicker ball late on and Carter soon sorted out Saggers, but Symonds is unbeaten on 124 overnight and appears to have single-handedly saved his side. Warwickshire have outplayed one of their nearest rivals but, having lost the whole first day and likely to lose much of the last, will almost certainly have to settle for a draw, a fate to which that woman with giant tattoos on her giant and wantonly exposed breasts who marched, swearing madly, through the drizzle up Sydenham High Street on Wednesday is almost certainly entirely indifferent.

Saturday, June 26th:

Kent 297 and 23 for 0.

MATCH DRAWN:
KENT 7 POINTS, WARWICKSHIRE 12.

A draw. Beckenham has become the ninth venue in Kent at which Warwickshire have drawn a championship match, following in the wake of Canterbury, Dartford, Dover, Folkestone, Gravesend, Maidstone, Tonbridge and Tunbridge Wells (the Bears won their only visit to Blackheath and lost each of their two matches at Catford and their 1947 visit to Gillingham). They have yet to play at Ruckinge, Drellingore or Snave.

The Year of the Bear

Persistent drizzle torpedoed any hopes the Bears had of pressing home their advantage today. The follow-on was duly enforced after Sami edged a Tahir outswinger and Trott dawdled down a second run and was beaten by Bell's throw from third man. But Symonds' excellence alone had foiled the Bears. He ended unbeaten on 156 from 167 balls, a stark contrast to the other 10 batsmen who between them managed 115 runs from 291 balls. Hogg's 4 for 90 doubled his champo wicket-tally and the Bears will hope confidence floods back into him now. All that remained was a fascinating session in which Kent openers Carberry and Fulton gathered 23 runs from 17 overs. Fulton scored five from 57 balls before the thickening clouds finally obliged with a downpour.

Warwickshire have stretched their advantage over Kent to 33 points, building the pressure on Fulton's men to win their game in hand. Gloucestershire have sneaked into second place but they won't last the course. Worcestershire are fourth but Surrey (51 points behind) and Lancashire (52 behind with a game in hand) still appear the main threat if they build up a head of steam. And when the champo resumes in 25 days time it will be Surrey and Lancashire next. Interesting.

Now, which way's Sydenham High Street?

****

SCORECARD

Warwickshire 1st innings

MJ Powell	c Patel	b Trott	134
MA Wagh	c Symonds	b Trott	86
IJL Trott	c O'Brien	b Saggers	115
IR Bell	c Fulton	b Patel	49
JO Troughton	st O'Brien	b Patel	21
GB Hogg	c Symonds	b Patel	28
*DR Brown	not out		27
NM Carter	not out		1
Extras	(b 3, lb 6, nb 32)		41
		Total	**502**
			for 6 dec

T Frost, N Tahir and A Richardson did not bat.

v. Kent at Beckenham

FoW: 1-171, 2-354, 3-396, 4-436, 5-453, 6-490.

Mohammad Sami 25-3-111-0, Saggers 24-5-63-1, Trott 32-7-102-2, Symonds 8-3-26-0, Loudon 17-1-88-0, Patel 33-8-103-3.

Kent 1st innings

*DP Fulton	c Powell	b Tahir	15
MA Carberry	lbw	b Carter	13
ET Smith		b Tahir	2
A Symonds	not out		156
MJ Walker		b Hogg	21
AGR Loudon	c Trott	b Hogg	9
+NJ O'Brien	lbw	b Hogg	13
MM Patel		b Hogg	24
MJ Saggers		b Carter	0
Mohammad Sami	c Frost	b Tahir	18
BJ Trott	run out		0
Extras	(b 5, lb 3, w 6, nb 12)		26
	Total		**297**
			all out

FoW: 1-17, 2-22, 3-50, 4-86, 5-108, 6-146, 7-215, 8-218, 9-296, 10-297.

Carter 19-7-44-2, Brown 10-2-31-0, Tahir 9-2-50-3, Wagh 2-0-4-0, Richardson 11-3-55-0, Hogg 22.2-3-90-4, Bell 2-0-15-0.

Kent 2nd innings (following on)

*DP Fulton	not out	5
MA Carberry	not out	14
Extras	(nb 4)	4
	Total	**23**
		for 0

ET Smith, A Symonds, MJ Walker, AGR Loudon, NJ O'Brien, MM Patel, MJ Saggers, Mohammad Sami and BJ Trott did not bat.

Tahir 3-0-7-0, Brown 5-3-6-0, Richardson 6-4-4-0, Trott 3-2-6-0.

Umpires: JH Evans and P Willey.

The Year of the Bear

Lost to KENT by 10 runs, D/L method (totesport).
Beat SOMERSET by 7 wickets (T20).
Beat NORTHAMPTONSHIRE by 4 wickets (totesport).
Beat GLAMORGAN by 26 runs (T20).
Lost to WORCESTERSHIRE by 3 wickets (T20).
Beat ESSEX by 54 runs (totesport).
Lost to NORTHAMPTONSHIRE by 4 wickets (T20).
Beat GLOUCESTERSHIRE by losing fewer wickets
with scores level (T20).
Lost to WORCESTERSHIRE by 41 runs (C&G Trophy).
Lost to GLAMORGAN by 5 wickets (T20).

Next came an orgy of one-day cricket. Ten games in 19 days. The Bears enjoyed an upturn in the totesport league with two wins out of three. After a 10-run D/L defeat at Beckenham, they beat Northamptonshire by four wickets at Edgbaston thanks to another classic one-day knock (74 from 71 balls) from Hogg. He then turned bowling demon with 5 for 23 to demolish a dishevelled Essex.

After reaching the final of the inaugural Twenty20 in 2003 hopes were high again this time round but much of the Bears' cricket, particularly the batting, in the group matches matched the untidy weather. They scraped through thanks to a last-gasp win at Bristol which earned a quarter-final visit to Cardiff. That set up a huge one-day double-header with that match, on Monday, following the C&G Trophy semi-final with Worcestershire at Edgbaston on Saturday.

A sensational treble loomed in the minds of the most optimistic supporters but by Monday night the championship was the only silverware still in sight. In the C&G, Vikram Solanki's 126 lifted Worcestershire to 257 for 4 before the Bears' pursuit was torpedoed by astute captaincy from Ben Smith, impressive fielding and unlucky injuries to Trevor Penney and Jonathan Trott. Then in the Twenty20 the Bears failed to emulate their group victory in Cardiff as Glamorgan made short work of a target of 158 thanks to a brilliant 74 from 52 balls by former Bear David Hemp.

****

Ten

v Surrey
at Guildford

Wednesday, July 21st:

Warwickshire 390 for 5.

Warwickshire played some scrappy cricket in the Twenty20. They continue to struggle in the totesport League and have just suffered a heartbreaking C&G Trophy semi-final defeat. So all that together stirred a few hopes amongst their pursuers in the championship that the Bears might be about to slide. They've shot their bolt. Peaked too early. That was the theory.

Those pursuers were no doubt much encouraged today when they consulted Teletext at lunchtime and discovered that, on the traditionally batsman-friendly pastures of Guildford, the Bears were wobbling at 112 for 3. And the formidable Knight was one of the three down. A dodgy foundation.

Less encouraging for those pursuers, but to the delight of the Bears' travelling supporters, was the close-of-play score. Warwickshire 390 for 5, sitting pretty having fought back superbly and, almost inevitably, adjusted a record or two along the way.

The Bears endured a difficult start in more ways than one. Traffic congestion gummed them up so badly on the way from the hotel to the ground that the start of play was delayed for 15 minutes. Then, horror of horrors, Knight actually lost a toss, although the blow was ameliorated when Surrey skipper Jon Batty bizarrely chose to field. The Bears were certainly going to bat, if Knight had called correctly.

Batty's thinking was that if there was to be any help at all for the bowlers it would be early on, especially with the morning overcast. Sure enough the new ball did a bit and it was just such a contuberance that did for Wagh, who edged his seventh ball to slip. Knight looked in fantastic form and hurried to 36 from only 41 deliveries but fatally edged a back-foot drive. Trott took 19 balls to get of the mark then started to motor before top-edging a pull at Phil Sampson to mid-off. 112 for 3. Surrey sensed they were on to something. But Bell and Powell took complete command with Bell in particular batting wonderfully. Come late afternoon it was 326 for 3 and Surrey were totally subjugated.

Bell's was the archetypal number three's innings. Called to the crease in the second over he first steadied the innings and contained the bowlers, then tamed and finally punished them. When Bell bats like this it really does seem anything's possible for him. Such speed and certainty of shot-selection. Instinctive footwork. Immaculate judgment outside off-stump. His on-driving of the seamers was the stuff of textbooks while he dealt with spinner Nayan Doshi (son of former Bears spinner Dilip) with near disdain.

With every boundary - and there were many - that thundered over the ropes of this elegant venue, any vestige of self-doubt the Bears might have collected during their glut of one-dayers evaporated further. This was batting of the highest order. Bell and Powell (voracious on the pull and hardly less fluent than his partner) added 214 to equal the record partnership for any wicket in first-class cricket at Guildford. That record they now share with another pair of Bears - Trevor Penney and Dominic Ostler - whose 214 stand frustrated an attack of Martin Bicknell, Joey Benjamin, Mark Feltham, James Boiling and Jason Robinson in 1992. It's also Warwickshire's best fourth-wicket offering against Surrey, surpassing the 188 taken by Alvin Kallicharran and Mike Smith off an attack, which could certainly be described as being no mugs, of Geoff Arnold, Robin Jackman, Graham Roope, Pat Pocock and Intikhab Alam, at Edgbaston in 1972.

v. Surrey at Guilford

Bell was within 55 runs of 1,000 in a season for the first time (he should still make it!) when his gorgeous innings ended on 155 from 238 balls with 24 fours. He received a rich ovation. Powell, meanwhile, completed back-to-back championship centuries with 106 from 145 balls with 13 fours before he was trapped in front by the persevering Sampson. But the partnership had sent the most emphatic messages around the country. No way the shot bolt.

In the last hour Brown re-acquainted himself with a crease of which he will always hold fond memories. It was here 10 years ago almost to the day that he first strode out to bat in the championship for Warwickshire - and immediately registered the sort of innings that was to become his trademark. Back in '94 the debutant went in at number 10 with his team in deep trouble at 131 for 8 against an attack of Cameron Cuffy, Joey Benjamin, Tony Pigott, Adam Hollioake and Andrew Smith and struck a gritty 54. (In terms of grit, mind, he was immediately shown up to be a mere pretender when, in the second innings, one of the great gritmeisters of all time, Andy Moles, acquired 203 in 562 minutes - at the time the slowest double-century in championship history.)

Anyway, tonight Brown saw the last session through as the shadows lengthened on the south London suburbs. He closed on 39 and looked in the mood to emulate Bell and Powell tomorrow. The Bears arrived here desperate to reaffirm their authority in the championship and no-one is more desperate than Douglas Robert Brown.

Thursday, July 22nd:

Warwickshire 537. Surrey 307 for 9.

Emulate Bell and Powell Brown duly did, to set up another excellent day for Warwickshire, despite the inevitable resistance of Mark Ramprakash.

Brown and Hogg still clearly like batting with each other and after the loss of nightwatchman Tahir this morning they biffed the Surrey attack to all parts. Hogg delivered a dynamic cameo, driving furiously for 67 from 41 balls with 13 fours. Brown rode his luck a bit, particularly through the slip area, but fully deserved his ton and ended with 106 from 145 balls with 17 fours. Although the Bears' tail for once folded swiftly the total of 537 is the highest in first-class cricket at Guildford.

The Bears are clearly a unit full of confidence, focus and togetherness. Their opponents appear chronically devoid of each of those qualities and apart from the resolute Ramprakash, their batting was ragged. Gazing up at 500-plus you've got a right to expect your openers to get their heads down, but Scott Newman flashed fecklessly at Pretorius in the third over and Rikki Clarke scored at a one-day rate of knots before playing on to Brown.

While Ramprakash set about boosting his average against Warwickshire (before this innings it languished at a miserable 134 over his last 10 innings) a succession of partners came and went with varying degrees of carelessness. None lasted an hour. Yet again Tahir showed that happy knack of striking in his first over. His first ball veered away to snare Alistair Brown and he also later ousted Tim Murtagh and Sampson in the first over of spells. Richardson undid the potentially adhesive Batty and forced Azhar Mahmood to play on, while Adam Hollioake thumped a run-a-ball 33 before falling to a wonderful catch by Powell on the mid-wicket boundary. Ormond, too, attacked briefly before attacking once too often.

It amounted to a smorgasbord of inappropriate batting and Warwickshire picked bits off the menu at regular intervals. You could only admire Ramprakash. How ironic that a man with Middlesex roots should form the lone source of Surrey application. His judgment outside off-stump, where enough deliveries jumped to be a menace, was beyond reproach. His 69th first-class century arrived just before the close and he alone of the home side could take any crumb of pride from this day.

Warwickshire, on the other hand, will head for their cosy pits tonight with much of the hard work done towards accomplishing home and away championship victories over Surrey for the first time since 1968 when Alan Smith's Bears secured a pair of eight-wicket triumphs in a fortnight. The elder statesmen of Section 19 no doubt fondly recalled, over their pints tonight, how back in '68 match figures of 63.2-29-109-11 from Tom Cartwright set up a comfy win at Edgbaston before a gritty 56 (the top score in the match) by Neal Abberley and 13 wickets from Lance Gibbs and Jack Bannister set up a similar pasting at The Oval.

Friday, July 23rd:

Surrey 331 and 363 for 7.

After a fascinating, fluctuating day the Bears still have a bit to do. Again some Surrey players were guilty of shots that would have had Bobby Abel shaking his head in disbelief but others, notably Batty, showed the thou-shalt-not-pass mentality that underpinned The Guvnor's 27,609 first-class runs for his beloved county. And, to the relief of the host club, they stretched the contest into its fourth day.

This morning Warwickshire appeared set to seal victory inside three. After Tahir's first ball of the day (remarkably he took four wickets in the innings, all in the first over of spells) ended Doshi's stubborn resistance, Surrey followed on 206 behind and promptly slid to 24 for 3. Clarke will have a hard time explaining why he left a Brown delivery which hit leg-stump. Pretorius struck a massive blow by swinging one into Ramprakash and removing the barnacle before it had time to get cemented. Buoyed by that, the South African, who bowled so well against this lot at Edgbaston, also ousted Newman via another flamboyant flash outside off-stump. Thoughts began to turn to a Saturday off.

Brown and Batty were not thinking along those lines though and highlighted the folly of their colleagues by knuckling down. In contrasting styles they wore down a bowling attack lacking that extra venom required to pierce correct batting on a good pitch. Hopes that Hogg had turned the corner after his wickets at Beckenham proved empty. His single first-innings wicket had arrived via a catch on the boundary and again today he appeared unlikely to give the close men anything to do, beyond take evasive action. Brown and Batty added 200 in 47 overs and Brown completed a powerful century from 129 balls with 16 fours and a six but then, to the Bears' giant relief, perished next ball. It was Tahir who got him, fortuitously, as Frost did well to take a feathered glance down the leg side.

The Year of the Bear

If that was lucky, Tahir's next wicket was fully merited. He beat Mahmood numerous times outside off-stump before finally getting the edge. When Brown quickly ended another unimpressive effort from Hollioake, Surrey were only 63 ahead with six men out.

Cue another fluctuation as Murtagh joined his skipper to add 94 in the last session. You could only admire Batty's defiance. If he knew his hold on the leadership was doomed he was going to make damned sure nobody could look back and say 'well where were your runs?' While he was there a route out of trouble remained for Surrey and when he safely defended the penultimate ball of the day, his 256th faced in five hours 20 minutes batting, it looked as if plotting how to dislodge him would occupy most of the Bears' thoughts tonight. But in went Pretorius one last time. The ball was quick, swung in a fraction and eluded Batty's tired defensive push. Up went the finger and Surrey closed at effectively 157 for 7 with only the bowlers left to bat.

Saturday, July 24th:

Surrey 412. Warwickshire 207 for 3.

WARWICKSHIRE WON BY 7 WICKETS. WARWICKSHIRE 22 POINTS, SURREY 6.

Job done. Calmly. Professionally. Skilfully. Warwickshire are 41 points clear at the top of the table. Just as important is the psychological ballast they have taken from this game - and the discouragement it's meted out to those pursuers.

The significance of Pretorius' late strike last night was emphasised this morning when Surrey's last three wickets added only 49. Murtagh reached a worthy 50 but was then superbly held caught and bowled by Brown. Doshi again showed he can bat but then got it all wrong with a horrendous heave at Hogg. Sampson became Tahir's seventh victim of the match and while match figures of 7 for 147 are not normally the sort to write home about, on this occasion they don't tell the story. Without Tahir's ability to nip out a wicket here and there the Bears would not have won.

Warwickshire were left with a target of 207 and most of the

final day to get it on a pitch playing as well as ever. There was just a tinge of alarm when Wagh played on attempting to leave a ball from Ormond and then Knight edged into the slips but Bell and Trott played it perfectly. Watchful at first, they asserted themselves gradually to add 138 in 34 overs and take their team to the brink of victory - and a giant step nearer the title.

After Trott perished for 61 from 100 balls - consistently resolute and pugnacious, he has been to the Bears this summer what Ralph Coates was to the Tottenham Hotspur midfield in the 1970s - a little contrivance could have allowed Bell to make a century in each innings. But he wasn't bothered about that and when victory arrived he was unbeaten on 96 from 146 balls with 11 fours plus a six flicked impudently over the marquees off Doshi. The double over Surrey was complete and while the boys of 1968 did it with a pair of eight-wicket drubbings, a brace of seven-wicket victories is not too shabby.

****

SCORECARD

Warwickshire 1st innings

*NV Knight	c A. Mahmood	b Ormond	36
MA Wagh	c Clarke	b Sampson	0
IR Bell	c Murtagh	b Doshi	155
IJL Trott	c Brown	b Sampson	25
MJ Powell	lbw	b Sampson	110
DR Brown	c Clarke	b Sampson	106
N Tahir	c Batty	b Ormond	4
GB Hogg	c Newman	b Doshi	67
+T Frost	lbw	b Sampson	0
A Richardson	c Newman	b Doshi	1
D Pretorius	not out		4
Extras	(b 10, lb 11, w 4, nb 4)		29
		Total	**537**
			all out

FoW: 1-6, 2-48, 3-112, 4-326, 5-376, 6-398, 7-505, 8-506, 9-529, 10-537.

The Year of the Bear

Ormond 31-7-90-2, Sampson 24.1-121-5, Murtagh 26-4-105-0, Azhar Mahmood 20-3-78-0, Doshi 25-0-101-3, Hollioake 4-0-21-0.

Surrey 1st innings

SA Newman	c Frost	b Pretorius	9
R Clarke		b Brown	21
MR Ramprakash	not out		145
AD Brown	c Frost	b Tahir	25
*+JN Batty	c Frost	b Richardson	1
AJ Hollioake	c Powell	b Hogg	33
Azhar Mahmood		b Richardson	25
TJ Murtagh	c Wagh	b Tahir	0
J Ormond	c Trott	b Brown	30
PJ Sampson		b Tahir	1
ND Doshi	c Bell	b Tahir	22
Extras	(lb 10, w 1, nb 8)		19
		Total	**331**
			all out

FoW: 1-10, 2-38, 3-102, 4-111, 5-183, 6-232, 7-233, 8-283, 9-288, 10-331.

Pretorius 19-2-73-1, Brown 16-4-57-2, Bell 2-0-11-0, Richardson 19-4-62-2, Tahir 11.1-2-63-4, Hogg 8-0-46-1, Wagh 3-0-9-0.

Surrey 2nd innings (following on)

SA Newman	c Trott	b Pretorius	13
R Clarke		b Brown	6
MR Ramprakash	lbw	b Pretorius	1
AD Brown	c Frost	b Tahir	103
*+JN Batty	lbw	b Pretorius	145
Azhar Mahmood	c Frost	b Tahir	14
AJ Hollioake	lbw	b Brown	9
TJ Murtagh		c & b Brown	57
J Ormond	not out		12
ND Doshi	st Frost	b Hogg	18
PJ Sampson	c Wagh	b Tahir	1
Extras	b 4, lb 15, w 4, nb 10)		33
		Total	**412**
			all out

v. Surrey at Guilford

FoW: 1-14, 2-15, 3-24, 4-224, 5-252, 6-269, 7-363, 8-377, 9-411, 10-412.

Pretorius 18-4-71-3, Brown 25-3-80-3, Tahir 18.3-1-84-3, Richardson 12-3-39-0, Hogg 13-2-48-1, Wagh 15-1-41-0, Bell 5-0-22-0, Trott 1-0-8-0.

Warwickshire 2nd innings (target 207)

*NV Knight	c Clarke	b Sampson	21
MA Wagh		b Ormond	4
IR Bell	not out		96
IJL Trott	c Batty	b Clarke	61
MJ Powell	not out		12
Extras	(b 2, lb 3, nb 8)		13
		Total	**207**
			for 3

DR Brown, GB Hogg, +T Frost, N Tahir, A Richardson and D Pretorius did not bat.

FoW: 1-15, 2-37, 3-175.

Ormond 13-4-37-1, Azhar Mahmood 11-1-40-0, Sampson 8-3-19-1, Murtagh 6-2-22-0, Doshi 10-1-37-0, Hollioake 2-0-12-0, Clarke 2-0-22-1, Brown 3.3-0-13-0.

Umpires: MJ Harris and VA Holder.

****

The Year of the Bear

Lost to SURREY by 90 runs (totesport).
Lost to LANCASHIRE by 2 wickets (totesport).

All-conquering in the championship, so why so poor in the one-day league? Relegation was starting to loom after a pair of away defeats which, for different reasons, left coach and captain furious. At Guildford, Surrey were allowed to pile up 315 for 8 (Brown 9-0-75-2, Richardson 9-0-76-1) to set up a straightforward victory, which even Bell's brilliant 89 from 70 balls could not avert. It was not so straightforward for Lancashire at Old Trafford, just two wickets the margin, but some scruffy cricket from his men in the field left Knight experiencing a new emotion in his short reign as captain: rage. Some slapstick fielding and dilatory changing round between overs which cost a six-run penalty triggered a withering post-match dressing-down for his team from Knight. The gist: if that sort of slapdash work imbues the Bears' four-day cricket the championship dream could still go pear-shaped.

****

Eleven

v Lancashire
at Old Trafford

Wednesday, July 28th:

Warwickshire 308 for 4.

The secret of a team destined for success is that somebody always delivers when the going gets tough. Not always the same body, but somebody. It's the essence of a winning side and applies to every sport whether it's cricket, football, rugby, hockey, dominoes, volleyball, cheese skittles or river-widening.

Say players A, B and C are the main men. Usually they will come up with the goods. At least two of them will deliver, often all three. But on the rare occasions when A, B and C all fail then, in a successful team, players D and E come up with the goods. Or if E also misses out, player F steps up to the plate and, with D, escorts the team from crisis.

Sometimes it will be players A, C and F who do the necessary. Sometimes B, D and E. Or just A and E. Or C and F. But one thing's for sure, somebody always delivers and even in the remarkable event of players A, B, C, D, E and F all enduring a collective off-day you can bet your bottom dollar that, in a side destined for success, players G and H get stuck in. And even then player I is invariably at his best when the chips are down, while players J and K have risen to plenty of occasions in their time. And player L is just the sort you would want alongside you in the trenches. Somebody

123

always delivers. That's why there's no panic when the opposition gets on top. And that's the way it has been for Warwickshire this season, as proved again at Old Trafford today.

With Knight's hairdryer treatment still fresh in the memory from the night before, the Bears won the toss, batted on a placid surface and promptly declined to 92 for 4. Knight and Wagh reached 72 without loss with barely a false shot but then fell in successive overs, both in irritating fashion. Knight will long wonder how he managed to edge behind to supply medium-pace trundler Mark Chilton with his first wicket of the season. Wagh cruised imperiously to 41 from 74 balls then, beaten in the flight, chipped a return catch to Gary Keedy just as a repeat of his big ton against this lot at Stratford appeared to beckon. Trott chipped a catch to short extra and Powell fell lbw trying to sweep his third ball. So it was down to players C and F.

After their runs at Guildford, Bell and Brown could hardly be in better form and they continued in the same vein. Keedy was dangerous, obtaining turn and looping the ball teasingly, but he was played with consummate care. So patient was Bell that at one stage he batted 14 overs without scoring, but it was not a case of a batsman becalmed and hanging on at the crease. It was simply one who intended to bat until the close of play and if that required outright defence in the short term then so be it.

Beyond Keedy, Lancashire's bowlers failed to exert enough pressure. Dominic Cork squandered almost as much energy on harmless short deliveries as Sami had at Beckenham last month, while Glen Chapple and Sajid Mahmood looked significantly either sides of their peaks.

After taking 140 balls over his first 50, Bell required only another 80 for his second by which time Brown had already reached three figures. Especially severe on Mahmood, the all-rounder scored at a crisp enough rate to allow his partner to play an unflustered anchor role. It was perfect partnership batting. By the time Brown lifted an obliging long-hop from Chris Schofield for six to reach his century, the alliance had comfortably exceeded Warwickshire's previous fifth-wicket best against Lancashire (191 by Dennis Amiss and Paul Smith on the same ground 20 years earlier). When they accepted an offer of bad light 25 minutes

v. Lancashire at Old Trafford

before the close, the partnership stood at 216 (Bell 106, Brown 120) with power to add tomorrow. A classy salvage operation was complete.

Thursday, July 29th:

Warwickshire 410. Lancashire 167 for 3.

At few sporting venues this side of Vladivostok can you have a rummage in a bargain book bucket before the action starts and come up with breathtaking value, like the autobiography of Richard and Judy for a mere ten pence. Such a deal was struck by one lucky punter at Old Trafford this morning and the way things turned out he was fortunate to have the tome in his possession. As the day unfolded, spectators needed something to take their minds off the cricket which yielded only 269 runs and little colour.

Lancashire fought back strongly this morning as Warwickshire's last six wickets fell for 64 runs. The partnership of Bell and Brown closed at 254 (the highest in all first-class cricket at Old Trafford) when the former edged a corker from Cork. It was far from the only good 'un that the former England seamer unleashed in an aggressive and well-directed spell from the Stretford End. He softened up Hogg with two bouncers then speared one in full to win an lbw decision, and if Cork had bowled like that 24 hours earlier to back up Keedy's good work, Lancashire would probably be well on top in this match.

The spinner returned to find Frost's edge and then at last end Brown's innings at 162 from 317 balls with 20 fours and two sixes. A late flurry from Richardson included one cover-drive the like of which Don Bradman could, frankly, only have aspired to, but the scorecard showed how heavily the Bears had leaned on C and F. They contributed 274 while eight of their colleagues together managed 76.

Still, a total of 410 meant Lancashire had to score big runs quickly but they were pegged back early on by accurate bowling and a stroke of bad luck. A yorker did for Chilton to supply Carter with his 100th first-class wicket. Then just as Loye was unfurling into offence he essayed a cut at Wagh, keeled over in pain and limped out of the match with a damaged Achilles.

Wagh sent down a 17-over spell that was unrewarded by wickets but cost only 25 runs to deny the home side the momentum they needed. Impressive stuff although he did have the benefit of bowling quite a lot at his fellow former Oxford blue Iain Sutcliffe. A former boxing blue, Sutcliffe effectively just put his guard up for the day, which didn't do his team's cause a fat lot of good.

Mongia chipped a return catch back to Hogg before Carl Hooper's cameo suggested why Lancashire have failed to live up to their tag as title favourites. The West Indian hit his second and fourth balls for sixes then tried to do the same to his 24th and found the safe hands of Brown at long-on. Hooper might have plenty of feathers in his cap in his long career already (when Ashley Giles made his first-class debut for Warwickshire against Kent at Canterbury in 1993 it was Hooper who dismissed him twice in the match - how often has he dined out on that?) but his team needed something bigger than 16 from him today.

At the close Sutcliffe was unbeaten on 67 from 61 overs and the match was interestingly poised after a not very interesting day.

Friday, July 30th:

Lancashire 412. Warwickshire 191 for 4.

Ever since Ian Bell first walked into the nets at Edgbaston at the age of 12 and started pinging the grown-ups' bowling to all parts it's been a matter of little dispute that his batting would give a lot of pleasure to a lot of people. Well, he's started in earnest. After three wonderful innings in Guildford and a technical masterclass in the first innings here, today he again batted beautifully. And as was the case in the first innings both here and at Guildford he did so under pressure.

The 22-year-old reached the crease this afternoon in the first over of Warwickshire's second innings with Lancashire buoyed by getting Knight early. By the close he had completed a century in each innings. During this match Bell's career average has crept above 40 for the first time, and it will stay there. Again he played Keedy magnificently. Rarely these days does a young English batsman emerge with an aptitude for playing spin but here's one.

Keedy, like Mushtaq Ahmed and Saqlain Mushtaq before him this season, was entirely mastered. It's an expertise that will serve Bell well in his long Test career ahead.

It's just as well for the Bears that Bell's reservoir of runs shows no sign of drying up. Lancashire have dominated all three mornings of this game so far, today through some rumbustious batting from Schofield and Chapple. After Sutcliffe's tortuous vigil ended at 72 from 217 balls in comic fashion when he offered no shot to a straight ball from Hogg, the two all-rounders made up for lost time by clattering 168 in 29 overs. Chapple once thraped a century off only 27 balls here against contrived Glamorgan bowling in 1993 (Matthew Maynard 6-0-110-1, Tony Cottey 6-0-121-0). That's a parcel of cricket from which nobody involved emerged with credit (at one stage Viv Richards, following the ball to the boundary, tried to kick it over the rope) but Chapple has shown over the years that he can lay into proper bowling as well, and today he thundered to a ton from only 82 balls. He lofted the ball with relish over the infield and in two cases, off Wagh and Hogg, also over the outfield. Knight abetted the onslaught with some unimaginative captaincy as he rotated Carter and Brown and his spinners but declined to use Tahir and Richardson at all. It seemed odd to allow numbers 10 and 11 to graze for hours when the ball was flying to all parts.

A morning session of 179 runs threatened to take the game away from Warwickshire as the home side galloped to 409 for 5, just a single behind. But remarkably the last five wickets folded for just three runs. Wagh accepted a slip catch to oust Schofield a single short of his maiden century and then took out the tail with a series of flighted straight balls. Does any other sport, apart from dominoes, fluctuate so wildly and unpredictably as cricket? Twenty minutes after appearing set to face a serious deficit - 78 perhaps, or 119 or 92 - the Bears went in again trailing by only two.

Knight steered his fifth ball to point then Wagh and Bell added 63 before the former was outfoxed by Keedy for the second time in the match. Bell and Trott built a methodical century partnership to shepherd the contest towards a draw but two wickets in the closing overs have kept Lancashire's hopes alive. Fifteen minutes from stumps Trott edged a good one from Keedy and then Powell completed the rare feat of bagging a pair, out third ball each time.

But still there was Bell. His ton arrived just before the close to warm applause from the knowledgeable Lancashire supporters. They probably knew it was the first time a Bears player had scored a century in each innings since David Hemp did so against Hampshire in 1997 and they probably also knew that Bell's was a far more creditable feat than Hemp's, as the latter's second ton in the game was achieved against bowling almost as inane as that on which Chapple gorged himself four years earlier.

Furthermore they almost certainly knew too that the most recent Bear to achieve the exploit against genuine bowling was Brian Lara against Leicestershire in the championship season of 1994. But how many of them knew that Bell was following in the hallowed footsteps first set down long ago by Septimus Kinneir, who became the very first Warwickshire player to score two centuries in a match, against Sussex at Chichester in the championship year of 1911?

Saturday, July 31st:

Warwickshire 353 for 7 declared.
Lancashire 194 for 4.

MATCH DRAWN.
LANCASHIRE 12 POINTS, WARWICKSHIRE 11.

For a few minutes this morning Lancashire had a sniff of victory. Nightwatchman Tahir fell lbw offering no stroke to Keedy and when Brown for once missed out, miscuing a pull to mid-on, Warwickshire were 213 ahead with four wickets remaining. If the home side could rifle through the tail. . . If the home side could get rid of Bell. . .

But they couldn't - and instead were left rueing a chance fluffed when Hogg, on two, fired a tough return catch back at Keedy but the spinner couldn't cling on. The lapse was expensive as the seventh-wicket pair eased the Bears out of trouble. Bell was still greedy for runs and fresh and organised enough to keep collecting them. Hogg steadied the ship by not only staying in but, as he has all summer, scoring runs at a brisk enough pace to alter the game

Ian Bell acknowledges the applause after reaching his century against Kent at Edgbaston, an innings many felt was his best yet.

The attitude and application of Michael Powell was exemplary all season. Left, he has just reached 50 against Kent at Edgbaston, then, below, he shows his annoyance at falling four short of a century.

Dougie Brown, above, crashes another four on the way to 49.

Another half century for Brad Hogg, right.

With plenty of time lost to the weather, only quick wickets could force a result for The Bears. But Kent had reached 229 for 1 before there was any real success, Michael Bevan, above, falling lbw to Carter for a duck as three wickets fell for two runs.
Below: Frost appeals for a stumping off Hogg.

Heath Streak's four wickets against Kent showed
encouraging signs of a return to fitness.

After a tough year, Jim Troughton hit back hard against Gloucestershire at Bristol with a century which hauled his side out of first-day trouble.

Above right: Troughton also impressed with the ball at Nevil Road, with 37 disciplined overs to rein in the home side's batsmen.

Below right: Craig Spearman took control though, here lifting another four runs towards his 237.

Left: Tony Frost - ever-present in the championship triumph, joined forces with Heath Streak to keep Sussex at bay on the final afternoon at Edgbaston.

Above: Heath Streak's input was restricted by injury but he impressed all at Edgbaston with his professionalism. And, in that partnership against Sussex with Tony Frost, he virtually sealed the championship triumph.

The Championship trophy
was flown to Worcester,
above, but had to
go back in its box after
the draw at New Road.
The insatiable Trott, left,
lodged two half-centuries
against the local rivals but
The Bears could not
force victory.

All the hard graft is rewarded as Nick Knight
accepts the championship trophy.

Above: Nick Knight celebrates with his fellow players,
rightly proud to be holding the trophy.

Below: After a job well done, the team have
a deserved shower in champagne.

v. Lancashire at Old Trafford

quickly. They added 117 before Bell, on 181 from 254 balls with 20 fours and a six, was run out by Cork. He departed cursing - he possesses the insatiability that drives all the best batsmen.

Hogg completed his sixth 50 in 11 championship innings (and took his batting average to 66) but the only question that remained was whether Knight would offer Lancashire any glimpse of victory with his declaration. The answer: not really as he set a target of 352 from 52 overs. Lancashire, with Loye unable to bat, had to start like a train and accelerate, but Brown rapidly disposed of both openers with the new ball. When the hard-working Carter collected the deserved wicket of Hooper, nicking a back-foot force, any chance of a serious run-chase vanished. Mongia took the chance to exhibit the range of his strokeplay not least, courtesy of Hogg, the ability to deposit long-hops to the boundary.

Warwickshire, still unbeaten in the champo, are 44 points clear with five games to play.

****

SCORECARD

Warwickshire 1st innings

*NV Knight	c Haynes	b Chilton	25
MA Wagh		c & b Keedy	41
IR Bell	c Hooper	b Cork	112
IJL Trott	c Hooper	b Keedy	9
MJ Powell	bw	b Keedy	0
DR Brown	c Chapple	b Keedy	162
GB Hogg	lbw	b Cork	0
+T Frost	c Haynes	b Keedy	6
NM Carter	c Haynes	b Mahmood	7
N Tahir	not out		12
A Richardson	c Hooper	b Schofield	17
Extras	(b 1, lb 7, w 1, nb 10)		19
		Total	**410**
			all out

FoW: 1-72, 2-78, 3-92, 4-92, 5-346, 6-346, 7-361, 8-368, 9-380, 10-410.

Chapple 26-5-73-0, Cork 27-6-53-2, Mahmood 25-4-100-1, Chilton 12-2-39-1, Keedy 40-7-109-5, Schofield 6.3-1-13-1, Hooper 7-1-15-0.

Lancashire 1st innings

MJ Chilton		b Carter	19
IJ Sutcliffe	lbw	b Hogg	72
MB Loye	retired hurt		44
D Mongia		c & b Hogg	15
*CL Hooper	c Brown	b Hogg	16
CP Schofield	c Wagh	b Carter	99
G Chapple	c Wagh	b Hogg	112
DG Cork		b Wagh	23
+JJ Haynes	lbw	b Wagh	0
SI Mahmood	not out		3
G Keedy	lbw	b Wagh	0
Extras	(b 1, lb 7, w 1)		9
		Total	**412**
			all out

FoW: 1-32, 2-130, 3-148, 4-190, 5-358, 6-409, 7-409, 8-412, 9-412, 10-412.

Carter 20-2-71-2, Brown 18-3-81-0, Wagh 30-7-86-3, Tahir 8-1-29-0, Hogg 25-2-107-4, Richardson 7-0-18-0, Bell 2-0-12-0.

Warwickshire 2nd innings

*NV Knight	c Keedy	b Cork	3
MA Wagh	c Haynes	b Keedy	24
IR Bell	run out		181
IJL Trott	c Cork	b Keedy	41
MJ Powell	c Cork	b Keedy	0
N Tahir	lbw	b Keedy	7
DR Brown	c Keedy	b Chapple	0
GB Hogg	not out		72
NM Carter	not out		3
Extras	(b 12, lb 2, nb 8)		22
		Total	**353**
			for 7 dec

v. Lancashire at Old Trafford

T Frost and A Richardson did not bat.

FoW: 1-3, 2-66, 3-184, 4-190, 5-214, 6-215, 7-332.

Chapple 17-1-68-1, Cork 9-2-24-1, Keedy 38-7-109-4, Mahmood 12-0-76-0, Schofield 11-0-43-0, Mongia 8-1-19-0.

Lancashire 2nd innings (target 352)

MJ Chilton		b Brown	20
IJ Sutcliffe	c Frost	b Brown	5
D Mongia	not out		108
*CL Hooper	c Trott	b Carter	11
CP Schofield		b Wagh	40
G Chapple	not out		5
Extras	(b 4, lb 1)		5
		Total	**194**
			for 4

MB Loye, +JJ Haynes, DG Cork, SI Mahmood and G Keedy did not bat.

FoW: 1-21, 2-34, 3-61, 4-178.

Brown 7-2-26-2, Carter 16-4-40-1, Wagh 15-4-56-1, Hogg 11-2-53-0, Tahir 3-1-14-0.

Umpires: IJ Gould and RA Kettleborough.

****

Beat NORTHAMPTONSHIRE by 1 wicket (totesport).

Hopes of survival in the totesport League rose with a thrilling victory, achieved with one ball to spare under the Wantage Road floodlights. Chasing a modest target of 172 the Bears made hard work of it at 0 for 1, 62 for 4 and 133 for 7 but Frost and Richardson scrambled them home in the final over.

Next up in the championship a Kent side in indifferent form but still with a theoretical chance of catching Knight's men.

****

Twelve

v Kent
at Edgbaston

Wednesday, August 11th:

Warwickshire 338 for 4.

In his previous four visits to the crease in championship cricket Ian Bell had struck 155, 96 not out, 112 and 181. Not bad. But today he somehow raised the bar again. His 121 was not the biggest, the longest or the most pressurised innings of that sequence but in terms of, as they say on telly, cricket shots, it was the best. In fact, you'd be hard-pushed to unearth a more accomplished innings this season.

Bell was soon called upon this morning when Knight, having struck Ian Butler for three successive fours, played on to the New Zealander. When, eight minutes later, Wagh failed to get his plates close enough to a ball he had viewed with aggression, the Bears were 29 for 2. After winning the toss, it was a poor start. But Bell and Trott were unfazed. Trott batted well but Bell, to the approval of a good crowd (including long-time Warwickshire-watcher Paul Merson), was on a different plane. So perfect was his timing that forward defensives sped further than the middled drive of many a lesser cricketer. His straight and on-driving was - and this is a risky label to impart - perfect. Bell's first 50 spanned just 52 deliveries and contained 11 fours.

v. Kent at Edgbaston

The unassuming Princethorpe College old boy would be the first to acknowledge that he was assisted by Kent's bowlers serving up a few pies. But it was still easy to embrace the notion that the spectators were watching the early work of a player whose paw-prints will be all over the record-books for county and country by the time he hangs up his boots in 2026. In this form, Bell's speed and execution of shot-selection is awesome.

Despite the disruption of a couple of showers, Bell and Trott added 138 in 27 overs before Min Patel produced a humdinger to take Trott's edge. The batsman stalked off grumpily - but then he always does. Trott hates getting out, which is one of the reasons he generally gets a few runs before it happens. Powell settled in but Warwickshire's supporters continued to enjoy the shimmering resonance of Bell's batting. He reached his sixth century of the season - strangely his first at Edgbaston - and sped on to 121 in two hours 56 minutes from 144 balls with 23 boundaries before, to the surprise of all present and the disappointment of all except the Kent party, he got out. He leaned back to cut the off-spin of Alex Loudon and bottom-edged the ball into his stumps.

Bell's was an innings of such quality, certainty and purity of stroke that whatever followed had to be an anti-climax. And it was. But what followed was more solid, important work propelling the Bears just that little bit further along the road to the county championship. Bell's departure left Warwickshire at 234 for 4 - a clatter then could have put Kent in charge. Instead Powell and Brown closed out the day in the Bears' favour with a partnership of wizened efficiency that is unbroken at 104.

Worthy stuff - but the question under discussion in the Tom Dollery after the close was this: Was Bell's innings the best ever by a Warwickshire player against Kent? One or two reckoned so. Others advocated Tiger Smith's destructive 173, full of crunching leg-side shots, at Edgbaston in 1928 until it was pointed out that Smith had built it against a Kent side deprived of Tich Freeman by England duty. Nick Knight's 174 in the championship-clinching contest at Canterbury in 1995 got a mention in dispatches. As did Alan Richardson's ice-nerved unbeaten 10 against Martin Saggers and Peter Trego in full flight at Edgbaston in 2003. But most votes went to Rohan Kanhai for his sublime 107 against Derek Underwood on a bunsen at Gravesend in 1970. Underwood was at his most predatory and took 14 wickets in the match, but met his match in Kanhai who nonchalantly got off the mark with a six and hit two more as well as nine fours as he dealt with every spitting cobra Underwood released at him. Bell's knock today stands third - behind Kanhai and Richardson.

Thursday, August 12th:

Warwickshire 457. Kent 135 for 0.

Not often during this happy season have Warwickshire endured a terrible session. Today they did. They slipped in a stinker between lunch and tea and it says much for their title aspirations that in the long run it probably won't matter a jot. Kent openers David Fulton and Ed Smith were busy gorging themselves on some wretched bowling that was haemorrhaging boundaries at the rate of one per over when just before tea a rainstorm broke. No further play, allied to a forecast for further rain, meant that the Bears' worst session of cricket this season will almost certainly cost them nothing.

First up, Brown and Powell both sliced into the slips early on but Hogg, in his last championship appearance of the season, signed off in characteristic style with 63 from only 60 balls. Yet again the Australian played an innings that shaped the immediate course of the match. With Frost contributing a feisty 25 from 35 balls, the Bears' lodged their tenth successive 400-plus first innings. And instead of setting out in pursuit of a reasonable but not dominating 350-odd, Kent were looking up at 457 and knowing they had no time to spare.

Mind you, with the pile of old socks that the Bears then served up, they wouldn't have needed much time if the rain had not arrived. Fulton and Smith did not have to take the slightest risk to rattle along at more than five an over. Streak was back but looking rusty, while Carter went for 41 in his first five overs. Smith took five fours from Tahir's first over and 25 overs had brought 26 fours and 135 runs when the clouds, to the considerable relief of Knight & Co, gave forth. What was that Napoleon said about lucky generals?

v. Kent at Edgbaston

An early finish then - and the question under discussion in the Tom Dollery was this: Was that the most abject cricket ever registered by Warwickshire against Kent? Apparently not. The final match of 1992, Andy Lloyd's last as captain, when Trevor Ward, Mark Benson and Carl Hooper hoisted Kent to 487 for 3 on the opening day, sprang immediately to a few minds. Someone suggested Gravesend, June 21st, 1946, when Peter Cranmer's side lost 15 wickets in 195 minutes on the final afternoon to lose by an innings despite a third of the match being lost to rain. But the tribulations at Tonbridge in 1913 took the honours. Even this afternoon's limp teamwork appears sturdy compared to the supine manner in which Warwickshire surrendered that day, all out for 16 in just 62 balls to the admittedly not-half-bad pairing of Frank Woolley and Colin Blythe.

Friday, August 13th:

Kent 255 for 5.

Mightily did the clouds continue to give forth last night and into the early hours of the morning. For hour upon hour, rain thundered into the canal towpaths snaking through Birmingham city centre (Birmingham has more miles of canal than Venice y'know - 35 to 26). The deluge streamed along the gutters of Acocks Green and Bordesley and rattled upon the roof of doomed Pebble Mill. It dismayed anyone who had left their washing out in Washwood Heath, drenched the stray cats in Nuneaton and Bedworth and turned the elfin glades of Stoneleigh into a mosaic of glistening shades of green, broken only by the occasional white flash of a furtive badger. And at Edgbaston it waterlogged the run-ups at the Pavilion End.

So waterlogged were they that although the rain stopped well before the scheduled 11a.m. start, cricket did not begin until 4p.m. Conditions were deemed too dangerous. One could only hazard a guess as to what Sir Alec Bedser would have made of it. Bedser, of course, famously bowled the Bears to defeat in a single day in May 1953 when the The Oval was so saturated that he trimmed his even modest run-up to a couple of paces and promptly recorded 13.5-4-18-8 to whip Warwickshire all out for 45. Surrey then scored 146,

135

bowled the Bears out for 52 (Bedser 13.4-7-17-4, Jim Laker 13-6-29-5) and it was all over within 10 minutes of the extra half-hour. An enthralling day during which masters of their craft gave a full exhibition of their mastery before a mesmerised crowd. Had it been 2004 not a ball would have been bowled.

There was no such improvised masterclass today as the esteemed cricketers were, until 4p.m., protected from the hazardous, nay treacherous, business of moving about on wet grass. Instead, with 64 overs lost in the day, Kent resumed after tea with four sessions to go and the Bears certain to take another step towards that title. In fact there's a small chance they could make it a big step after the visitors lost five wickets this evening. Fulton and Smith added another 49 before Tahir, showing considerable character after his ordeal yesterday, deservedly ousted the latter, caught at short-extra. Fulton and Loudon added 45 but when the captain, seconds after reaching his 25th first-class century, was deceived by Wagh's flight, he was briskly followed back to the hutch by two colleagues. Michael Bevan was bowled offering no shot to Carter, then Matthew Walker edged a big turner from Wagh. When Matthew Dennington perished to the last ball of the day - a rapid yorker from Streak - Kent were still 53 adrift of the follow-on and need Loudon, 27 not out overnight, to hang around some more tomorrow.

Saturday, August 14th:

Kent 420. Warwickshire 123 for 2.

MATCH DRAWN.
WARWICKSHIRE 12 POINTS, KENT 12.

He did. Loudon hung around plenty long enough to not only shepherd his side to a draw, but reinforce John Inverarity's belief that he would make a jolly good signing for the Bears.

Loudon found an aggressive partner in Niall O'Brien. The Irishman had a narrow escape before he had scored when Brown failed to hang on to a sharp chance close in off Wagh, but then capitalised on it brutally. Kent's tradition of productive wicket-keeper batsmen is considerable and O'Brien, only in the team due to Geraint Jones' absence with England, maintained it nobly. Positive at all times, he cleared the ropes on four occasions and the follow-on figure was briskly attained as O'Brien and Loudon added 127 in 29 overs to make the draw a certainty. O'Brien reached 69 from 83 balls before he nicked a hook at Streak who, showing encouraging signs of a return to fitness, also had Patel well snaffled in the slips later in the over and then Butler caught behind. When Loudon's polished 231-minute stay and Trott's embryonic 27-minute tenure both ended with catches by Frost the wicket-keeper had five victims in the innings and Warwickshire possessed a lead of 37. As the Bears players filtered through the pavilion gate Hogg left the Edgbaston championship scene forever nursing a batting average 66.20 and a bowling average of 62.92.

Just as in the meeting of these sides at Beckenham, the final throes were gloriously pointless. Knight's first run took him to 1,000 for the season for the fifth time, but by the time he reached yet another half-century the attention of most spectators had strayed to the "roller coaster of emotion" (football cliché 47b) that was Oldham Athletic v Walsall in League One. Radios all over Edgbaston were alive with the news that from 2-0 up, the Saddlers had gone 4-2 down, pulled it back to 4-3 then had a goal wrongly disallowed and instead of finishing 4-4 let another one in and lost 5-3. Oh yes, and Warwickshire need 53 points from their last four games to be sure of the championship.

****

SCORECARD

Warwickshire 1st innings

*NV Knight		b Butler	18
MA Wagh	c O'Brien	b Butler	5
IR Bell		b Loudon	121
IJL Trott	c O'Brien	b Patel	50
MJ Powell	c Fulton	b Butler	96
DR Brown	c Fulton	b Butler	49
GB Hogg	c Smith	b Patel	63
HH Streak		b Joseph	2
+T Frost	c Joseph	b Trott	25
NM Carter	c Fulton	b Dennington	0
N Tahir	not out		3
Extras	(b 6, lb 9, w 4, nb 6)		25
		Total	**457**
			all out

FoW: 1-22, 2-29, 3-167, 4-234, 5-339, 6-394, 7-397, 8-439, 9-439, 10-457.

Butler 24-3-114-4, Joseph 18-4-83-1, Trott 13-0-67-1, Dennington 15-1-60-1, Patel 23.2-0-31-1, Loudon 9-2-31-1, Walker 7-0-21-0, Bevan 3-0-9-0.

Kent 1st innings

*DP Fulton	st Frost	b Wagh	100
ET Smith	c Wagh	b Tahir	95
AGR Loudon	c Frost	b Carter	92
MG Bevan	bw	b Carter	0
MJ Walker	c Trott	b Wagh	1
MJ Dennington	lbw	b Streak	16
+NJ O'Brien	c Frost	b Streak	69
MM Patel	c Wagh	b Streak	0
IG Butler	c Frost	b Streak	2
RH Joseph	not out		19
BJ Trott	c Frost	b Bell	4
Extras	(b 4, lb 9, w 1, nb 8)		22
		Total	**420**
			all out

v. Kent at Edgbaston

FoW: 1-184, 2-229, 3-230, 4-231, 5-255, 6-382, 7-382, 8-390, 9-406, 10-420.

Streak 23-4-85-4, Carter 19-4-85-2, Brown 11-1-52-0, Tahir 15-1-71-1, Hogg 20-1-58-0, Wagh 18-4-55-2, Bell 0.4-0-1-1.

Warwickshire 2nd innings

*NV Knight	not out		63
MA Wagh		b Loudon	33
HH Streak	c O'Brien	b Loudon	11
IJL Trott	not out		1
Extras	(b 1, nb 14)		15
		Total	**123**
			for 2 dec

IR Bell, MJ Powell, DR Brown, GB Hogg, +T Frost, NM Carter and N Tahir did not bat.

FoW: 1-79, 2-115.

Butler 4-0-21-0, Joseph 6-0-24-0, Trott 6-3-13-0, Loudon 12-2-30-2, Dennington 5-0-29-0, Walker 3-1-5-0.

Umpires: B Dudleston and MJ Kitchen.

****

Beat KENT by six wickets (totesport).
NO RESULT v Gloucestershire (totesport).

The totesport revival continued with a stroll to victory over Kent set up right at the top of the game by Streak blasting out batsmen one, two and three in his first three overs. Warwickshire are still playing catch-up though, and it was more a case of two points dropped than two gained when rain arrived to abort the floodlit tussle at Edgbaston with Gloucestershire with the Bears 31 for 2 in the eighth over chasing 192 in 42.

****

Thirteen

v Gloucestershire
at Bristol

Thursday, August 19th:

Warwickshire 350. Gloucestershire 20 for 0.

The County Ground, Bristol, should ooze history. Some of the greatest names of all - W.G. Grace, Gilbert Jessop, Wally Hammond, Jim Foat - conducted their glorious careers here. A generous share of genius has been sprinkled upon this land. Wonderful games and momentous exploits have unfolded here. Yet look around it now and it oozes about as much history as a milk bottle.

Nevil Road is the most charmless county ground by a mile. It is functional, bare and bland. Pictures of great figures hang on walls but the walls are in charmless buildings unworthy of a site of such special sporting interest. The lack of respect for heritage is summed up perfectly by the crass rechristening of the structures at either end of the ground. The Messier-Dowty Grace Pavilion and the Marston Pedigree Jessop Stand. Class.

The Bears have not travelled down here on a history trip though. They are here to keep Gloucestershire - 47 points behind them with four games to go - at bay and they will have to do it without key men. Bell has finally got his Test call and today made his England debut in the last Test against the West Indies at The Oval. Hogg has joined up with Australia to prepare for the ICC Champions Trophy.

v. Gloucestershire at Bristol

Heath Streak is playing but with a groin twinge he suffered in Tuesday's totesport League washout. Streak won't be fit to bowl until later in the match but Inverarity and Knight plumped for his experience batting at eight rather than risk giving 22-year-old batsman Ian Westwood his debut in a pressure match on a pitch that usually helps the bowlers. They changed their minds late on. Westwood was told on Tuesday he would be playing here but half an hour before play began this morning he learned he would be carrying the drinks instead. Dewald Pretorius and Jim Troughton are recalled so the Bears have still only used 15 players this season.

The toss was a foregone conclusion - the Bears have won nine out of 12, Gloucestershire have lost nine out of 12. Sure enough, Knight called correctly and Warwickshire batted. But then, as has happened surprisingly often despite this runfest of a summer, at first things didn't go at all to plan.

Jon Lewis is a bowler the Bears know plenty about - enough to have told Gloucestershire they intend to try to sign him at the end of the season. For almost a decade Lewis has been collecting championship wickets with regularity - Warwickshire's Wasim Khan was his first nine years ago this month - and he took less than two overs this morning to add Knight to the list when the Bears captain was acrobatically held by Mark Hardinges at second slip. After Wagh lifted carelessly to square-leg and Powell played away from his body, it was 38 for 3. Then Trott nicked a waft at Hardinges and it was an inauspicious 78 for 4.

The Bears have been in similar discomfort before on away territory this season - at Horsham, Guildford and Old Trafford - and salvaged the situation. This time Troughton and Brown were the rescuers with an abrasive counter-attack, which brought 182 runs in 43 overs. After a psychologically bruising year, Troughton was due a bit of fortune and he enjoyed some early on against the moving ball, but he also played some wonderful trademark drives. He lunched on 43, reached 50 from 104 balls with his 10th four and then joined in the applause for Brown's 50, from 56 balls. It was impressive work by the pair yet largely unobserved by their team-mates, who were gathered round a goggle-box in the dressing room watching Bell take to Test cricket like a duck to water.

The Year of the Bear

A four and three off successive deliveries from the spin of Ian Fisher took Troughton to a century. It was a knock that gave pleasure to a lot of people who shared the left-hander's angst at his difficulties since his premature sortie into England's one-day unit last summer. This was his first ton since then and it was a big one for the Bears, bailing them out before, on 120 from 228 balls with 19 fours, Troughton fell in strange fashion. He swept Fisher only for Craig Spearman, at slip, to spot the shot early and run around to intercept the ball on the leg side.

Brown was only nine short of his third century in five innings when he slashed Roger Sillence to gully. His 91, including 19 fours and a five, came from 117 balls - a tasty scoring rate that summed up another typical dogged Dougie innings. A *Braveheart*-type scenario. And how refreshing to see a five go down in the book, only Warwickshire's second of the season. There just aren't enough fives around in county cricket these days.

Troughton and Brown's partnership snared yet another record. It was the Bears' 27th century stand of the season, surpassing the county's previous record of 26 lodged in 1993. But after they departed, just like before they arrived, the Bears made a bit of porridge of dealing with an attack composed principally of prosaic seam. Streak nurdled 29 to help justify his selection primarily as a batsman but at 313 for 9 two batting points appeared destined for the Swanee. Not so. Tahir and Pretorius combined judicious playing and missing with alert running and the occasional slog to inch the total towards 350. A scrambled leg-bye raised the 37 stand and that precious fourth batting point.

Unusually, though, the Bears have not posted a massive score first dig. Gloucestershire survived five overs with no alarms against a Streakless attack and know a good day tomorrow would put Warwickshire under pressure.

v. Gloucestershire at Bristol

Friday, August 20th:

Gloucestershire 352 for 3.

Watching Phillip Weston bat is an exercise that tends to make attention stray, so while he was grinding his way to 30 at one run per over this morning a tall, bespectacled, lank-haired, pot-bellied spectator, high in the Jessop Stand, gazed out across the grass and let his imagination attempt to wring some evocation from the sterility that is 2004 Nevil Road.

He tried to picture the massive bearded figure of Grace out there in the middle helping a full toss deliberately bowled by Somerset's Sammy Woods (who had received a signal from the scorer that Grace was on 98) to the leg-side boundary to become the first player to score 100 first-class hundreds. He tried his best to imagine the spectators of 1924 applauding and joshing and hurling their hats high in the air as Hammond hammered Middlesex to all parts for a match-winning unbeaten 174, on a terrible wicket on which the two teams' first innings combined had mustered just 105. He tried to conjure the image of the great Tom Goddard wrapping his huge hands round the ball ready to release another six off-spinners of immaculate length and flight, or the ball making a two-second journey to the fence from the angelic blade of Zaheer Abbas, or Jim Foat prowling in the covers in a rain-affected John Player League game.

But no. Nothing came. Perhaps it was the remorseless grind of noise from the building site away to the left, but images of heroism and grandeur failed to intrude upon the stark reality of Weston tucking another two to backward square leg.

Watching Spearman bat was more interesting though and Warwickshire were forced to do it all day. The New Zealander resumed this morning on 11 and will resume tomorrow morning on 232 having become the first Gloucestershire batsman to make a double-ton at their Bristol HQ since Wally Hammond against Somerset in 1946.

With Streak restricted to fielding duties the Bears' bowlers were reduced to persevering in hope. Spearman should have gone on 136 when Pretorius rapped him half-forward right in front but was staggered to have his appeal turned down. On 219 the New Zealander slashed Brown hard to gully where Trott couldn't cling on to a tracer. But basically Spearman did much as he pleased, cutting, sweeping and pulling his way to 23 fours and four sixes. Troughton was the pick of the bowlers and ended the day with 17-5-48-1, highly respectable figures in the light of the onslaught. He sent back Michael Hussey after defeating a sweep and maintained good control all day. Tahir had dismissed Weston courtesy of Trott's sharp slip catch but the young bowler then got some stick and was not called upon at all in the last two sessions. Pretorius removed Ian Fisher caught behind, but that was in the 59th over and skippers generally like their strike bowlers to strike a bit earlier than that.

Spearman batted with great care late on, apparently determined to still be there at the close ready to start all over again tomorrow. Such was his determination that an offer of bad light was accepted at quarter to six, 12 overs before the close. The new ball was due but with Spearman past 200, Gidman ticking over sweetly on 40, Gloucestershire in front and Warwickshire looking knackered and resigned it seemed an odd decision to say the least.

Saturday, August 21st:

Gloucestershire 592 for 8 declared.
Warwickshire 111 for 1.

Warwickshire went into this match sizing up Gloucestershire as potential challengers for the title. Such is the condensed nature of the First Division, though, that Gloucestershire could still get relegated and it became abundantly clear today that it's that end of the table on which their minds are focused. A draw with full bonus points here would make them virtually safe from the drop. So they batted on - and on and on and on. They have ensured they will achieve the requisite draw, and altered a few records along the way, but it hardly made for compelling cricket or a great advertisement for a two-division championship. True, when it was one league of 17 or 18 there were plenty of, in league table terms,

v. Gloucestershire at Bristol

meaningless late-season games but if relegation issues encourage this sort of safety-first mentality then let's have 13th v 15th in a duel to see who might finish 11th every time.

The Bears had a pleasant early surprise when Spearman perished in the day's seventh over. He drove hard off the back foot and Troughton clutched an excellent return catch low to his right to end the Kiwi's innings at 237 from 279 balls in five hours 43 minutes with 25 fours and four sixes. With Gidman already out, caught at short-leg off Wagh, Gloucestershire were 368 for 5 with two new batsmen in. Time perhaps, to go through the lower order like a ferret down a rabbit 'ole.

Not so. Chris Taylor and Steve Adshead added 59 and after Brown bowled them both, off stump and leg stump respectively in quick succession, Hardinges and Sillence, hardly names to strike fear into bowlers, enjoyed themselves hugely. They swung merrily and saw off the spinners, the new ball and the belated entry into the attack of Streak. As the score piled up, 500 came and went and Sillence twice cleared the ropes, some of the home supporters clapped and cheered without inhibition. Others, aware that every passing over chipped away at their team's chances of winning the game, asked each other whether a declaration might come some time this century. A venerable chap in a cloth cap speculated that Taylor, Bristol-born and Gloucestershire through and through, had decided to exact some retribution for 1936 when Bob Wyatt's Bears came here and scored 336 runs in 207.5 overs in their two innings. Spinners Goddard and Sinfield between them sent down 170.5 overs for 203 runs and even Warwickshire president Sir Charles Hyde described the drastic rearguard action as "a blot on cricket". Was this revenge?

At 570, the total became Gloucestershire's biggest against the Bears, bettering their 569 off the not-half-bad attack of Shaun Pollock, Tim Munton, Gladstone Small, Dougie Brown, Neil Smith and Ashley Giles at Cheltenham in 1996. No declaration. At 581, Hardinges and Sillence had posted Gloucestershire's best eighth-wicket stand against Warwickshire, consigning to the dustbin of former records the 146 lodged by Billy Neale and George Lambert in 1947. Still no declaration. Even when, at 588, Sillence finally fell lbw to Trott - the ninth bowler used - still no declaration. The innings was allowed to drag on for another 13 minutes before Taylor finally declared after 161 overs.

Gloucestershire had gambled on the long shot of their ability to bowl Warwickshire out again but after three balls of the Bears' second innings it appeared Taylor had been right all along. Knight got only half-forward to Lewis and was bowled with his team still 242 in arrears. Wagh should have gone for nought too but Adshead dropped him off James Averis.

In the last 90 minutes of the day came an hour of gripping cricket. Lewis asked plenty of testing questions and Sillence sent down a lively spell from the Pavilion End. But Wagh and Trott applied themselves. Trott, in at three because Powell was still nursing a bruised knee sustained at short leg from a pull by Taylor, got lucky on 20 when all present, apart from the umpire, noticed he had nicked one from Lewis. Unaffected, he kept his nut down until the close and Gloucestershire were denied further success. Both batsmen reached their half-centuries just before stumps - Wagh from 73 balls, Trott from 99 - which were deserved reward for correct and strong-minded batting in increasing gloom. Warwickshire still need to bat most of tomorrow but their cricket post-tea was the sort of gritty, uncompromising work, denying the opposition just when they thought their chance had arrived, of which championship triumphs are made.

Sunday, August 22nd:

Warwickshire 308 for 8.

MATCH DRAWN.
GLOUCESTERSHIRE 12 POINTS,
WARWICKSHIRE 10.

Warwickshire's summer has been littered with batting exploits. The road to the title had been adorned by a triple-century, a double-century and 14 centuries so far but today, when that road got seriously windy and troublesome it was an innings of 11 that stood tall. Rarely, down the years, have 11s been the stuff of legend. Today's, from Naqaash Tahir, fell into that category.

v. Gloucestershire at Bristol

It provided a fascinating and, for Warwickshire's supporters, jubilant conclusion to a match that had drifted laboriously at times and in which the Bears looked jaded most of the time. Today their rearguard action faltered either side of lunch and Warwickshire were only 39 runs ahead with three wickets left and 30 overs still to go when Tahir joined Brown at the crease. Gloucestershire had kept nicking a wicket here and a wicket there to move within sight of ending the Bears' unbeaten record. Get Brown or Tahir and they just had Carter (on a pair) and Pretorius (did well to last 44 minutes first innings but you wouldn't back him to repeat the feat) to come.

Brown had already manacled himself to the crease and was at his most obstreperous. Frost and Streak had between them consumed 129 minutes. But Brown needed one more staunch ally. Tahir came over all staunch. Gloucestershire knew from the first innings he could bat a bit - now they discovered he is an unflappable sort of chap too. For over after over, he played each ball on his merits. Leaving one, blocking one, leaving one, blocking one.

When he reached the crease, four slips and a gully waited to pounce. Within a couple of overs every single fielder was round the bat. Tahir had 22 eyes burrowing into him from just yards away, trying to dig out an error. But no. Leave, block, block, leave. Hardly a false shot.

Between every over Tahir and Brown met in the middle. Jockeying each other along. Keep going. Keep going. Brown inched to 30 and stayed there for 44 balls. Tahir was on eight for 34 balls. Seven successive overs did not yield a run. By the time Brown drove Gidman into the hands of Taylor at short extra and departed for 49 in three hours 29 minutes, the Bears were 64 ahead with 12 overs remaining.

Fifteen minutes later, with six overs left and the lead 66, Taylor offered a handshake. Tahir's 11, from 68 balls, had spanned 88 minutes of implacable defiance. Richly did Section 19 applaud. It was arguably the finest unbeaten 11 ever recorded for Warwickshire, although some might argue the case for Freddie Calthorpe's unflappable innings against Derbyshire at Derby in 1928 when he saw the Bears' pursuit of 176 in less than two hours through to a triumphant conclusion with just five minutes to spare. Others would perhaps cite Steve Perryman's skilful and lion-hearted resistance against Richard Hadlee and

The Year of the Bear

Clive Rice in their devastating pomp for Nottinghamshire at Trent Bridge in 1978, when the tail-ender defied like a Trojan while the Bears folded for 56 and 81 all out. But Tahir's is in the frame, no question.

Wagh and Trott had major shares in the escape too for keeping Gloucestershire at bay last night. Both departed annoyed with themselves this morning though, Wagh having yet again edged behind and Trott having yet again failed to build a half-century into the full monty. When they fell in successive overs just before lunch the home side sensed their chance. When Powell and Troughton fell in successive overs after lunch they sensed a big chance. Then when Frost and Streak departed in quick succession Gloucestershire had their main chance. But in Tahir, it transpired, alongside the mighty Brown, Warwickshire had the trump card. The four points earned for the draw give Sussex, who already had a Herculean task to catch the Bears, a Herculean task with knobs on.

****

SCORECARD

Warwickshire 1st innings

*NV Knight	c Hardinges	b Lewis	7
MA Wagh	c Gidman	b Averis	17
MJ Powell	c Hussey	b Lewis	10
IJL Trott	c Adshead	b Hardinges	21
JO Troughton	c Spearman	b Fisher	120
DR Brown	c Hussey	b Sillence	91
+T Frost	c Taylor	b Sillence	2
HH Streak	c Spearman	b Fisher	29
NM Carter	c Hardinges	b Fisher	0
N Tahir	not out		18
D Pretorius	c Weston	b Lewis	9
Extras	(b 1, lb 10, w 1, nb 14)		26
		Total	**350**
			all out

FoW: 1-10, 2-38, 3-38, 4-78, 5-260, 6-266, 7-300, 8-300, 9-313, 10-350.

148

v. Gloucestershire at Bristol

Lewis 23-7-59-3, Averis 18-3-89-1, Hardinges 17-2-78-1, Gidman 5-1-21-0, Sillence 14-4-50-2, Fisher 20-5-42-3.

Gloucestershire 1st innings

CM Spearman		c &b Troughton	237
WPC Weston	c Trott	b Tahir	30
MEK Hussey	lbw	b Troughton	26
ID Fisher	c Frost	b Pretorius	13
APR Gidman	c Powell	b Wagh	47
*CG Taylor		b Brown	30
+SJ Adshead		b Brown	32
MA Hardinges	not out		68
RJ Sillence	bw	b Trott	92
JMM Averis	not out		0
Extras	(b 3, lb 11, w 1, nb 2)		17
		Total	**592**
			for 8 dec

J Lewis did not bat.

FoW: 1-99, 2-190, 3-229, 4-363, 5-368, 6-427, 7-434, 8-588.

Pretorius 20-2-84-1, Carter 23-1-93-0, Brown 31-9-84-2, Tahir 5-0-43-1, Wagh 28-3-107-1, Troughton 37-9-106-2, Powell 7-0-36-0, Streak 8-1-24-0, Trott 2-1-1-1.

Warwickshire 2nd innings

*NV Knight		b Lewis	0
MA Wagh	c Adshead	b Averis	73
IJL Trott	c Spearman	b Fisher	79
JO Troughton	lbw	b Fisher	21
MJ Powell	c Weston	b Sillence	9
DR Brown	c Taylor	b Gidman	49
+T Frost		b Lewis	28
HH Streak	c Hardinges	b Lewis	4
N Tahir	not out		11
NM Carter	not out		0
Extras	(b 5, lb 3, w 2, nb 24)		34
		Total	**308**
			for 8

D Pretorius did not bat.

FoW: 1-0, 2-163, 3-164, 4-202, 5-202, 6-263, 7-281, 8-306.

Lewis 27-6-89-3, Averis 15-4-57-1, Hardinges 13-2-42-0, Sillence 17-8-33-1, Fisher 36-20-50-2, Hussey 1-0-1-0, Taylor 1-0-2-0, Gidman 12-4-26-1.

Umpires: A Clarkson and NJ Llong.

****

Fourteen

v Sussex
at Edgbaston

Tuesday, August 24th:

Warwickshire 177 for 2.

The strange and congested nature of the First Division was perfectly illustrated by Sussex's situation going into this match. They alone, with their game in hand, can still deprive Warwickshire of the title. But they could also still be relegated. Their likely finishing position is somewhere between the two but Chris Adams' team - and most notably Mushtaq Ahmed - has hit form. Last season they finished on fire to overhaul Surrey in the final straight - if they beat the Bears here a similar climax will beckon.

Privately, Sussex reckon if they win here they will go on to win the championship. Warwickshire's recent stuttering has been noted. But they have left it late. Very late. If the Bears avoid defeat here the championship is all but theirs and after a rain-affected first day Sussex will have to go like the clappers to inflict defeat on them now.

Forty-four overs were lost in the day and between the showers the two prime architects of the Bears' success this season - Knight and Bell - did the business again. They batted extremely well, as they had to in the face of a fierce examination by the best county attack in the country. Wagh soon edged a good one from Mohammad Akram, after which it was battle joined between Knight and Bell and Akram and Kirtley. Four fine exponents of their craft locking horns. It was a conflict worthy of a five-figure crowd rather than one, in terms of non-members, barely into three figures. Ceefax and Cricinfo were no doubt in overdrive but why not get along? Maybe it's the counties' fault. Gate receipts are so negligible now wouldn't it be worth reducing admission to two or three quid just to draw people in and make days like this the occasions they should be?

Kirtley was most impressive, making the batsmen play and beating Bell several times early on. But Knight batted with the focus and restraint of a man who knew that if he could play one more long innings here it would take his side to the brink of the title. He faced 62 balls before hitting a four. When the opening bowlers had a rest, Mushtaq probed and tweaked and grunted and whooped as he resumed his marathon of a contest with Bell at Horsham. Once again Bell, fresh from rave reviews for his 70 on Test debut, played the spinner imperturbably, only once defeated, on 40, when he failed to detect a googly and survived a huge lbw appeal.

As the second-wicket pair dug in, assisted by a couple of showers, Sussex plugged away with discipline. Robin Martin-Jenkins rarely erred in his stock-bowling role, though when he dropped a fraction short Bell pulled him into the Hollies Stand. Knight and Bell added 130 in 41 overs before Knight fell just as Wagh had, lured into playing at a swift away-cutter. In mediocre light, Sussex pressed hard for another couple of wickets but Bell was matched for resolve and concentration by Trott in the last hour. A taut day's cricket ended with the Bears, just, ascendant.

Wednesday, August 25th:

Warwickshire 346. Sussex 125 for 1.

Today Sussex looked like the champions they are. And Warwickshire looked like the nervous pretenders to the crown they are.

It will still take a hell of an effort for Sussex to acquire the win they need here, but they bowled with such collective nous and batted with such purpose that they still have a fingerhold on their title. Stranger things have happened in this wacky old sport.

v. Sussex at Edgbaston

Crucially, Sussex got Bell early this morning. England's newest recruit added only three to his overnight 84 before he left a ball from Kirtley and lost his off-bail. Akram soon added the scalp of Powell, undone by bounce, then Troughton steered Kirtley to point. When Brown pulled Martin-Jenkins to mid-on the Bears were 226 for 6 and regretting that the man who had so often steered them out of such choppy waters this season - Hogg - was away with Australia.

Trott, however, trails Knight and Bell only marginally in significance to Warwickshire's success this season and he would not be moved. He passed 50 for the ninth time this summer and, having lost three partners in quick succession, found his fourth more resolute. Sussex grew sick of the sight of Frost at Horsham - again here he defied them, not just protecting his wicket but punishing the rare loose offerings that came his way. The seventh-wicket pair added 99 - and most importantly occupied most of a session - before Trott left the gate open and departed smouldering at yet again failing to convert 50 into 100. His demise triggered a rapid dissolution of the tail - something that has happened infrequently to the Bears this season and is further evidence that their momentum is dwindling.

In reply to 346, Sussex openers Richard Montgomerie and Ian Ward rattled up 100 in 25 overs. The clouds lifted so the ball swung less, but the batters were also abetted by some pretty moderate bowling. Montgomerie, not normally a batsman to empty the bars, struck 11 fours in his first 50 from just 44 balls.

The Bears then tightened up. Brown, having gone for four fours in his first over, conceded only 20 runs from his next 10. Tahir showed he has the bottle to fight back from taking a bit of stick by ousting the well-set Ward with a yorker. But Cottey batted with the quiet confidence of a man at home in this pasture. He first trod this turf on championship duty 15 years and 51 weeks ago as a callow Glamorgan batsman when he played a vital part in his side's cliffhanger victory. Scores of one and three (twice sorted out by Allan Donald) by the 22-year-old batsman appeared negligible until the final thrilling afternoon when Warwickshire, chasing 194, were taken to the brink by a tenth-wicket stand of 82 between Gladstone Small and Norman Gifford. Finally Greg Thomas returned to trap Small lbw for 69 with the Bears within a big hit of victory on 189. Glamorgan won by four runs - how negligible were Cottey's one and three then?

Fifteen years and 51 weeks later he accompanied Montgomerie solidly to the close. Sussex are still in this game and this title equation. In dominoes terms, Warwickshire are in sight of a check-out but Sussex are charging up the final straight still in with a shout - and it's their drop.

Thursday, August 26th:

Sussex 482 for 9.

Somebody really should tell the cricket-lovers of Birmingham what's going on here. The two best teams in county cricket are fighting out what is almost certain to be a decisive duel in the championship race. The first day was truncated but compelling, the second and third have been intriguing. Plenty of Warwickshire members have turned up but where are the casual punters? The 1951 title triumph was watched by an average 5,389 spectators a day at Edgbaston. This season it's nearer to just the 89.

This morning's cricket was fascinating. Anyone wishing to see sixes over the wicket-keeper's head, chaotic running, leg-side wides or custard pies sailing through the air would have been disappointed, but for connoisseurs of intense, gritty, hard-fought cricket it was a treat. Sussex had to amass a big total and do it quickly. Warwickshire knew that if they could bowl Sussex out for anything around the 300-mark the title was virtually theirs. Nothing soft about this cricket.

The Bears had the better of the first session. Sussex made progress in the second and third. At the end of the day (the term used literally and not, in this case, as the hoary old cliché) Sussex know if they bowl well tomorrow they can win this match.

In the morning their batsmen were shackled by accurate bowling from Streak and Bell. Streak soon got rid of Montgomerie, then Cottey and Murray Goodwin added 46 slow runs. Too slow. The increasing pressure told when the third-wicket pair had differing views over a single and found themselves at the same end. Exit

Cottey from the Edgbaston crease for the last time. Adams' urgency to up the tempo was clear but cost him his wicket when Trott showed the reactions of a hummingbird to cling on to a screamer at slip off Pretorius.

It was a good morning's work by the Bears but after the first session yielded 77 runs in 35 overs, the second brought 161 in 36. Prior, reprieved by Trott at slip off Tahir on 21, drew Goodwin out of his shell and as Sussex moved in front the fielding became ragged. A spate of ground-fielding fumbles prompted Brown to boom: "Come on lads, we're all over the place." Sussex were showing the steel of Red Rum, Warwickshire the nerves of Crisp.

Bell, doing his international credentials no harm at all by showing he can bowl long, disciplined spells, returned to bowl Prior with his first ball back. Tahir usually contributes something and he nipped out Martin-Jenkins and Davis. At 412 for 9, with his side having a useful lead of 66, Adams might have declared to try and nip a couple out tonight but instead he let last pair Kirtley and Akram have a flail and they did so to good effect against a resigned-looking Bears unit. Kirtley lodged only his third first-class 50 and the tail-enders put on 70 by the close. They lifted the lead to 136 - very useful - and Adams will surely declare overnight but would he have been better off pulling out after tea and trying to damage the Bears' top-order?

Friday, August 27th:

**Sussex 482 for 9 declared.
Warwickshire 205 for 7.**

**MATCH DRAWN.
WARWICKSHIRE 10 POINTS, SUSSEX 12.**

The Bears are almost there. They now require 20 points from their last two games (against two teams likely to be relegated) to secure top spot. They are within touching distance of the title. And today they didn't half earn the right to be there. A fine Sussex side - worthy champions for the past year - tried everything they knew and twice appeared to have buckled the Bears beyond repair. But

The Year of the Bear

Tony Frost and Heath Streak stood firm in a final session of high tension. Sussex were denied the victory they deserved and which would have sent them into their game in hand full of belief. Instead as they packed their kit into the cars tonight you sensed they knew deep down that their chance had gone.

Adams declared overnight and when his pacemen promptly reduced Warwickshire to 15 for 3, it appeared the Sussex skipper had got his tactics spot on. Similarly, when just before tea the Bears were seven wickets down and still four runs behind with 35 overs left the game looked all over. But Warwickshire, as always this season, found heroes in the nick of time.

Kirtley and Akram used the new ball superbly this morning. Kirtley bowled Wagh through the gate. Akram did for Bell with one that kept low and had Trott caught at gully by one that reared up. 15 for 3. Or minus 121 for 3.

But have two men ever sold their wickets more dearly than Knight and Powell? Like Kinneir and Quaife - professional batsmen who simply hated getting out - these two got stuck in. They simply *had* to occupy some time. The ball passed the edge many times and once took it but Knight, on 15, saw Ward drop the catch off Akram. The fourth-wicket pair reached lunch intact.

The seamers had excelled but Sussex still had the little matter of Mushtaq to wheel away on a last-day wicket. Soon after lunch he cramped Knight on a pull and the Warwickshire skipper chopped on to his leg-stump. The strip was not deteriorating as Sussex had hoped though and it was the quicker men who again powered Sussex forward. Powell, on 39 from 106 balls, was left helpless by an Akram inswinger. Troughton ate up 87 valuable minutes but then lifted Martin-Jenkins to square-leg. When, on the stroke of tea, Brown edged a leg-break, the Bears were minus 4 for 7 with 35 overs left. And the weather fine.

Frost and Streak had to survive for at least an hour. Unflappably - as unflappably as Henry Fonzerelli himself - they did so. With Akram and Kirtley tiring and Martin-Jenkins unthreatening, Sussex looked more and more to the magic of Mushtaq. But slowly, steadily, the pressure lifted. Forty ahead. Fifty ahead. Then at 60 ahead came the over that probably marked the transition of Sussex from champs to ex-champs. Frost carved

v. Sussex at Edgbaston

Kirtley over point for six then socked fours through the covers and square-leg. Adams offered his hand. And the powers-that-be started making arrangements for the championship trophy to be physically removed from Hove.

****

SCORECARD

Warwickshire 1st innings

*NV Knight	c Ward	b Akram	65
MA Wagh	c Ward	b Akram	6
IR Bell		b Kirtley	87
IJL Trott		b Martin-Jenkins	90
MJ Powell	c Prior	b Akram	5
JO Troughton	c Martin-J	b Kirtley	2
DR Brown	c Adams	b Martin-Jenkins	12
+T Frost	lbw	b Mushtaq Ahmed	48
HH Streak	c Goodwin	b Martin-Jenkins	2
N Tahir	not out		3
D Pretorius	lbw	b Martin-Jenkins	14
Extras	(b 2, lb 6, nb 4)		12
		Total	**346**
			all out

FoW: 1-11, 2-141, 3-184, 4-195, 5-198, 6-226, 7-325, 8-327, 9-330, 10-346.

Akram 27-5-94-3, Kirtley 32-7-75-2, Mushtaq Ahmed 27-3-74-1, Martin-Jenkins 21-5-62-4, Davis 13-0-33-0.

Sussex 1st innings

IJ Ward	lbw	b Tahir	34
RR Montgomerie	lbw	b Streak	78
PA Cottey	run out		30
MW Goodwin	lbw	b Streak	75
*CJ Adams	c Trott	b Pretorius	7
+MJ Prior		b Bell	95
RSC Martin-J	c Frost	b Tahir	26
MJG Davis	c Frost	b Tahir	8

Mushtaq Ahmed	c Tahir	b Pretorius	21
RJ Kirtley	not out		53
M Akram	not out		35
Extras	(b 6, lb 14)		20
		Total	**482 for 9**
			dec

FoW: 1-106, 2-135, 3-181, 4-190, 5-293, 6-343, 7-363, 8-372, 9-412.

Streak 31-8-92-2, Pretorius 22-1-99-2, Brown 26-8-71-0, Tahir 10-3-24-0, Bell 24-4-57-1, Troughton 10-3-24-0, Powell 1-0-15-0, Wagh 5-0-23-1.

Warwickshire 2nd innings

*NV Knight		b Mushtaq Ahmed	23
MA Wagh		b Kirtley	0
IR Bell		b Akram	6
IJL Trott	c Goodwin	b Akram	0
MJ Powell	lbw	b Akram	39
JO Troughton	c Davis	b Martin-Jenkins	33
DR Brown	c Prior	b Mushtaq Ahmed	14
+T Frost	not out		45
HH Streak	not out		27
Extras	(b 4, lb 9, pen 5)		18
		Total	**205**
			for 7

N Tahir and D Pretorius did not bat.

FoW: 1-6, 2-15, 3-15, 4-66, 5-98, 6-121, 7-132.

Akram 20-6-45-3, Kirtley 21-5-68-1, Martin-Jenkins 14-6-20-1, Mushtaq Ahmed 31-13-52-2, Davis 3-2-2-0.

Umpires: GI Burgess and DJ Constant.

****

v. Sussex at Edgbaston

Beat GLAMORGAN by 4 wickets (totesport).

Warwickshire took advantage of Glamorgan, already crowned totesport League champs, fielding an understrength team. Spurred on by Hogg, who negotiated his release for the day from Australia's ICC Champions Trophy squad, they comfortably chased down a target of 211 with four overs to spare. Now could they clinch the big prize in the backyard of their biggest rivals?

****

Fifteen

v Worcestershire
at Worcester

Tuesday, August 31st:

Warwickshire 298 for 6.

This is the sort of contest the powers-that-be had in mind when they split the championship into two divisions. The theory; no more meetings between lowly counties with nothing riding on the outcome. Here, there is plenty riding on it. The Bears started this match knowing that 20 points against their closest rivals will clinch the championship. Worcestershire's objective is similarly urgent. If they don't win this game they will be relegated. All set then for cricket of substance and intensity. That's the theory.

But today, little more than tedium. It would be difficult - no, impossible - to dress this up as an attractive day's cricket. Connoisseurs of the forward defensive shot enjoyed a feast. For the rest of a good crowd at New Road it was cricket gruel.

Warwickshire won the toss - of course. It was their sixth successive won toss and Worcestershire's fifth successive lost one. In fact the pre-match coin action was the nearest the day got to entertaining as Steve Rhodes flipped the item of money skyward and it spiralled dramatically through the cool autumn air before surrendering to gravity, crashing to earth and, far from landing in conventional fashion with heads or tails gazing upward, first rolled in thrilling fashion along the pitch before toppling down in favour of Nick Knight.

v. Worcestershire at Worcester

Unsurprisingly, after that nerve-shredder, Knight was subdued when, minutes later, he started to bat. He progressed at precisely one run per over up to lunch to set the tone for a soporific day. Only briefly, after Wagh edged an Andy Bichel lifter into the slips, did the cricket escape mundanity. Ian Bell's first three scoring shots, in his first six balls faced, were perfectly timed boundaries straight and through the covers off Bichel. Bell's form remains regal and while Knight blocked stodgily, Bell applied barely more force yet so sweet was his touch that the ball raced away. He reached 50 from 67 balls with successive boundaries - his 10th and 11th - off Nadeem Malik.

Yet another Bell ton beckoned but in the second over after lunch he leaned back to force left-arm spinner Ray Price and chopped to Graeme Hick at slip. Price had caused problems from the moment he came on just before the interval and when, in his next over, he had Knight taken at bat-pad, Warwickshire were 117 for 3 and the optimists among the home members dared to hope. The realists were to be proved shrewd. On previous occasions this season the Bears have attacked their way ferociously and flamboyantly out of a hole. This time Jonathan Trott and Michael Powell did it the other way.

It was a perfect late-summer afternoon at the heavenly location that is New Road. The sun was strong, seagulls circled, corks were gently dislodged by spectators high in the Basil D'Oliviera Stand and cream teas were going down a treat in the Ladies Pavilion. This was the sort of scenario for which cricket-loving expats forced to work abroad as telecom engineers in Kuwait, trawler accessory salesmen in Iceland, parrot smugglers in South America or bamboo packers in Lombok spend long nights pining. To be in Worcester on such an afternoon makes all the rubbish in one's life worthwhile. To be here is enough. But still the cricket declined into such inertia this afternoon that of those people who had the honour of attending today, roughly half plumped for 40 winks.

Trott's desperation for another century - he has still converted only one of eight 50s into three-figures - rendered him almost strokeless. Powell was slightly more aggressive than his partner but still principally the old Powell; the pre-captaincy version who would rather hang upside down from a canal bridge in midwinter having crazed mallards peck at his nose than surrender his wicket.

The fifth-wicket pair added 131 in 49 overs. They saw off Price, who bowled accurately but with decreasing menace throughout the afternoon session, and wore down the seamers until, half an hour after tea, Powell mispulled Malik to mid-on. Trott had another seven overs left in him but that second century remained elusive when he drove Matt Mason to cover. His 63 took three hours 44 minutes and 182 balls - at that rate of knots, centuries do become more difficult to gather.

The 24-year-old had done another fine job for his team though, and although Brown soon edged the new ball into the slips the Bears ended the day in a decent position. Troughton concentrated hard and Tahir supplied a moribund day with a late flash of colour when he impudently smacked Bichel to the cover and long-leg ropes in the final over. Warwickshire played like a team that has done the hard work and now needs only to avoid catastrophe. Worcestershire look resigned to the drop.

Wednesday, September 1st:

Warwickshire 460. Worcestershire 161 for 3.

Another joy of coming to New Road is the chance that you might bump into Vanburn Holder patrolling his old patch. Sure enough Holder, a Worcestershire quickie for 12 years, tapped on the press-box windows this morning with a cheery: "Good morning gentlemen". He is not umpiring in this match so circulated the ground as full of *joie de vivre* as ever, without the slightest trace of shame and guilt from Edgbaston 1976 where, bowling for the West Indies against the Bears, he peppered poor, vulnerable tail-ender Bob Willis so persistently with short-pitched balls in dodgy light that he earned a rebuke from umpire Arthur Jepson (it's an incident that remains unique in the history of cricket - the only time that a bowler whose first Test match victim was Tom Graveney has been reprimanded by an umpire whose first clean sheet as Lincoln City's goalkeeper was against Leeds United).

v. Worcestershire at Worcester

How Worcestershire could have done with Holder in his pomp today. They badly needed to polish off the Bears' first innings quickly this morning but Bichel and Mason of Australia, Hall of South Africa and Price of Zimbabwe toiled away punchlessly. Troughton and Tahir were untroubled and extended their seventh-wicket partnership to 114 before Troughton edged Malik to depart for a well-organised 64 in 183 minutes. Tahir batted as though number eight in the order is where his future lies. He lifted Mason and Hall stylishly over the leg-side in-field and struck five other fours to move within a single of a maiden half-century, only to then edge Bichel to Rhodes. Even then the paucity of Worcestershire's attack was illustrated as Frost, Streak and Carter added 51 for the last two wickets.

Embarrassment loomed for the home side when they declined to 38 for 3 in the eighth over. Stephen Moore fell second-ball to a shooter from Brown, Peters was defeated by a Streak inswinger and Smith fell to a wonderful, two-handed diving catch by Powell at square-leg. At 58 for 3, still 253 short of the follow-on figure, at tea, Worcestershire were in trouble roughly as deep as the Marianas Trench (36,198 feet down on the floor of the Pacific Ocean by the way). But Hick had his deep-sea gear on. He thundered to 50 from 57 balls with eight fours and a six lifted into the pavilion off Brown and inspired Kadeer Ali who, after an uneasy start, was playing with as much aplomb as his partner towards the close.

Warwickshire missed a sitter when Hick, on 63, edged Troughton and Trott fumbled the chance at slip. That apart it was splendid defiance from the fourth-wicket pair. Hick closed on 78 and Kadeer on 56 - worthy stuff even though, in terms of Worcestershire's season, it amounts to little more than polishing the brasses on the Titanic.

In mid-afternoon the Bears looked odds-on to collect the championship in the next 48 hours - the trophy has been conveyed here - but unless they came unfurl some long-dormant bowling firepower it will stay in its box for a little while longer.

The Year of the Bear

Thursday, September 2nd:

Worcestershire 416. Warwickshire 94 for 3.

Before this season these two old neighbours had met 177 times in the championship. This contest makes it 179 and the two additions this summer probably consist of the most and least entertaining of the lot. The game at Edgbaston was a corker, catapulting one way then the other and careering to a result inside three days. This has been dreary in the extreme, plodding through session after session and plotting the predictable path to a draw that will keep Warwickshire waiting and send Worcestershire down.

It was straight into full plod mode this morning with the first 40 minutes yielding 21 runs as the two batsmen showed no inclination to get after Streak and Carter. Brown then came on to wake a few people up. He had Kadeer caught behind gloving a lifter in his first over and knocked out Hick's off and middle stumps with a daisy-cutter in his fourth.

Five wickets down and still 109 short of the follow-on figure, Worcestershire appeared in jeopardy but each batsman from six to ten held Warwickshire up for at least 50 minutes. Bichel batted positively before falling to an alert catch by Frost. Hall's leaden, 105-minute 26 ended with a smart slip catch by Trott before Price took his side past the follow-on with three successive fours off Troughton. Price then missed with a swish at Brown who celebrated only the third five-wicket haul by the Bears this season, following Streak's two in the match against Northamptonshire at Edgbaston.

Rhodes and Mason added 88 in contrasting styles. While Rhodes plodded, Mason finally lifted the cricket out of torpor with some good old-fashioned tail-end slogging. He smashed his way to 50 from only 40 balls before tea and went on to 63 from 56 with nine fours and three sixes before Streak ended the fun by removing the middle-stump. Malik lasted only three balls but the Bears went in second time around with their lead eroded to 44 by Mason's assault.

That advantage grew to 138 by the close. Knight and Wagh batted with freedom to add 66 in 15 overs before Knight sliced a sweep and Hick jogged backwards to take a simple catch. Wagh has signed a new four-year contract during this match and would have loved to celebrate it with his first century since June. But after collecting a fluent 40 from 66 balls he played fatally across the line to Price. Tahir, so impressive in the first innings, took only six balls to provide Hick with his first wicket of the season.

Something sensational has to happen tomorrow for this game to end in a result. Gloriously unpredictable though cricket can be, you wouldn't back against the contest plodding to a draw.

Friday, September 3rd:

**Warwickshire 254 for 8 declared.
Worcestershire 156 for 1.**

**MATCH DRAWN.
WORCESTERSHIRE 11 POINTS,
WARWICKSHIRE 11.**

Plod to a draw it duly did and the champo champagne stays on ice. Knight was never likely to set Worcestershire a generous target because a) why should he? and b) there's the salutary precedent of 1977. Back then at New Road the Bears bossed the game until the final afternoon when skipper David Brown, to the surprise of everybody and not least umpires David Evans and Douglas Sang Hue, offered the home side an attractive target of 270 in 280 minutes. They duly reached it - and a three-wicket victory - thanks to Alan Ormrod's ton. So Worcestershire could expect little generosity from Knight today. To avoid relegation they had to bowl the Bears out. And they weren't capable of it.

They enjoyed the early bonus of removing Bell, who bat-padded off Price, but then encountered the Implacable Twins for the second time in the match. Trott and Powell only batted 23 overs together but it was enough to grind Worcestershire's hopes of winning - and therefore staying up - to dust. Trott eked 51 from 121 balls and Powell 43 from 101. In this match the pair have resided at the crease for a combined 682 minutes - it seems longer.

The Year of the Bear

Price wheeled away at length again, taking his tally of overs bowled in the match to 91, as Warwickshire took their time to add 160 runs in 48 overs today before finally pulling out in mid-afternoon. The target: 299 from 38 overs. Worcestershire's corpse twitched as Moore and Hick biffed the ball about briefly, and Hick twice lifted Wagh into the New Road Stand, but it was academic. The contest meandered to a draw, which satisfied the Bears. Sussex, their only challengers now, are under huge pressure to win both of their games in hand, against Middlesex and Gloucestershire next week, and even if they did that they would have to win their last match, against Surrey, and hope the Bears falter at Northampton. The trophy remains in its box - but surely not for long.

****

SCORECARD

Warwickshire 1st innings

*NV Knight	c Smith	b Price	37
MA Wagh	c Peters	b Bichel	15
IR Bell	c Hick	b Price	54
IJL Trott	c Smith	b Mason	63
MJ Powell	c Price	b Malik	69
JO Troughton	c Rhodes	b Malik	64
DR Brown	c Hall	b Bichel	3
N Tahir	c Rhodes	b Bichel	49
+T Frost	lbw	b Bichel	19
HH Streak	not out		30
NM Carter		b Hall	13
Extras	(b 10, lb 19, w 9, nb 6)		44
		Total	**460**
			all out

FoW: 1-26, 2-108, 3-117, 4-248, 5-271, 6-274, 7-388, 8-409, 9-426, 10-460.

Mason 33-10-84-1, Bichel 29-5-108-4, Hall 24-7-74-1, Malik 16-3-68-2, Price 56-24-95-2, Ali 1-0-2-0.

v. Worcestershire at Worcester

Worcestershire 1st innings

SD Peters	lbw	b Streak	19
SC Moore	lbw	b Brown	0
GA Hick		b Brown	93
BF Smith	c Powell	b Streak	2
Kadeer Ali	c Frost	b Brown	66
AJ Bichel	c Frost	b Troughton	36
AJ Hall	c Trott	b Brown	26
*+SJ Rhodes	not out		44
RW Price		b Brown	32
MS Mason		b Streak	63
MN Malik		b Streak	0
Extras	(b 8, lb 14, nb 13)		35
		Total	**416**
			all out

FoW: 1-12, 2-30, 3-38, 4-195, 5-202, 6-254, 7-286, 8-322, 9-410, 10-416.

Streak 29.2-8-81-4, Brown 32-3-89-5, Tahir 8-0-48-0, Wagh 7-2-11-0, Carter 20-2-71-0, Troughton 25-6-76-1, Bell 2-0-18-0.

Warwickshire 2nd innings

*NV Knight	c Hick	b Price	39
MA Wagh		b Price	40
IR Bell	c Ali	b Price	17
N Tahir		b Hick	0
IJL Trott	c Rhodes	b Hall	51
MJ Powell		b Malik	43
JO Troughton	c Rhodes	b Price	6
Brown	not out		27
+T Frost	c Hall	b Malik	20
NM Carter	not out		1
Extras	(b 4, lb 5, w 1)		10
		Total	**254**
			for 8 dec

HH Streak did not bat.

FoW: 1-66, 2-93, 3-94, 4-108, 5-180, 6-193, 7-213, 8-243.

Mason 12-4-36-0, Bichel 11-1-47-0, Malik 13-1-54-2, Price 35-9-83-4, Hick 2-1-1-1, Hall 10-1-24-1.

Worcestershire 2nd innings (target 299)

SD Peters	c Troughton	b Streak	9
SC Moore	not out		83
GA Hick	not out		56
Extras	(lb 1, w 1, nb 6)		8
		Total	**156**
			for 1

BF Smith, Kadeer Ali, AJ Bichel, AJ Hall, *+SJ Rhodes, RW Price, MS Mason and MN Malik did not bat.

FoW: 1-14.

Streak 7-0-20-1, Brown 4-0-20-0, Tahir 2-0-16-0, Carter 3-0-35-0, Troughton 6-0-21-0, Wagh 6-1-33-0, Trott 1-0-10-0.

Umpires: MJ Harris and AA Jones.

****

LOST to GLOUCESTERSHIRE by three wickets (totesport).

A fateful Saturday for Warwickshire brought the defeat that ultimately sealed their relegation. Trott (70) and Bell (76) ensured a decent total of 248 for 7 but the Bears were unable to defend it. The home side sneaked home with four balls to spare to secure their First Division status and leave Warwickshire's at the mercy of other results. Those results, during the next three days, went the wrong way and the Bears were sentenced to play Second Division totesport League cricket in 2005.

A fateful day too for highly talented all-rounder Graham Wagg, whose random post-match drug test revealed traces of cocaine. The 22-year-old admitted the offence and, on October 18th, was banned from cricket for 15 months by the England and Wales Cricket Board. He was also sacked by Warwickshire.

****

Back in the championship, on the afternoon of Monday September 6th, Sussex lost to Middlesex by five wickets and the last challenger had fallen by the wayside. Warwickshire were the champions and they had done it with only 15 players, one of whom - Giles - had played only one game. Nick Knight's tightly knit bunch had followed in the footsteps of Frank Foster's, Tom Dollery's, A.C. Smith's and Dermot Reeve's. The Champs.

****

Sixteen

v Northamptonshire
at Northampton

Thursday, September 16th:

Warwickshire 276 for 8.

Warwickshire finally got their hands on the county championship trophy today - 10 days after securing it. And it was so apposite that their season of endeavour should reap its ultimate reward here at Northampton.

After a forgettable day's cricket, Nick Knight accepted the trophy from the man from Frizzell on the outfield just before 6pm. The sense of satisfaction and joy from every Bear-related person present - players, coaches, back-up staff, Section 19 - was deep. And the glow of the 2004 achievement mingled with a vivid sense of history, for here was Warwickshire's captain accepting the most important trophy of them all on the very spot where, almost a century earlier, the Bears sealed their very first championship triumph.

Yes it was here at Northampton, back in 1911, on the final day of a truly amazing season that the Bears, under the dynamic leadership of Frank Foster, broke the stranglehold of the 'Big Six'. That was the culmination of a remarkable tale and, if you'll pardon the digression, I think it's worth relating.

Such a wretched figure did Warwickshire cut in the opening match of 1911, against Surrey at The Oval, that their cricket was described by *Wisden*'s correspondent as "inexcusably weak".

v. Northamptonshire at Northampton

Surrey won by an innings and 46 runs, less than two hours into the second day, after Warwickshire folded pathetically for 62 and 87.

With a reluctant captain in Charlie Cowan and a team that had hardly picked up a bat or ball in practice, they resembled a rabble. Most significantly, they were reeling from the absence of their star player, the brilliant all-rounder Foster. When Warwickshire stepped out at the Oval, the maverick genius Foster was back in a Birmingham office having announced his retirement from cricket at the age of 22! Without him, Warwickshire were ruthlessly exposed by a half-strength Surrey side. Just two days into the season they were in disarray. A shambles. Yet 116 days later they were popping champagne corks. Foster had abandoned his ludicrous retirement to seize an ageing, disparate bunch of players by the scruff of the neck and shape them into champions.

In that first game, Warwickshire were an embarrassment to the city of Birmingham. After their last, at Northampton, they were mobbed by thousands at New Street station and fêted by his esteemed nibs the Earl of Warwick at a celebration dinner. Warwickshire's 1911 triumph remains among the most unlikely and remarkable in the history of sport. And it reached its crescendo on exactly this plot off Wantage Road in the warren of back-streets in east Northampton.

It is no exaggeration to say the success hinged entirely on Foster. Digbeth-born and Solihull-educated, this local boy had burst into county cricket in 1908 with a match-winning bowling performance at Derby and lit up every cricket field he subsequently trod. The son of William Foster, a cricket nut and Warwickshire committee member, Frank was a blistering batsman, brilliant slip fielder and left-arm bowler of pace and aggression.

For several years he dazzled in a struggling team. In 1908, 1909 and 1910 Warwickshire finished 12th, 12th and 14th of the 16 counties. Much of their cricket in the 'golden age' was rudderless and prosaic. Drastic action was required to jolt the county side out of drift and in January 1911, the committee came over all adventurous. After four captains in three years, the team desperately needed stability and leadership but all Warwickshire's experienced players were professionals - and you couldn't have one of *them* leading the side. It had to be an amateur. So young Foster was asked. He agreed. Then he changed his mind and announced his retirement.

So Warwickshire arrived at the Oval with naval officer Cowan in charge. He promptly navigated the team to a wretched defeat and bagged a pair to boot. Cowan added his voice to the renewed clamour: "We must persuade Frank."

Foster was again heavily lobbied, not least by his father, had a change of heart and the seed of a sensational story was sown.

Warwickshire's second match was against Lancashire at Old Trafford. It was another tough away assignment but Foster got busy. He called all the players - amateurs and professionals - together to hammer home the team ethic. So ingrained was the class system in cricket that amateurs (toffs who played the game when it suited them) and professionals (who earned their living from cricket, paid by the county club) ate, travelled and changed separately. From now on, Foster insisted, on the field at least, togetherness must be everything.

Secondly, he called for positive cricket at all times. "The bat should always beat the hands of the clock," he insisted. "If the batsmen can't manage 61 runs per hour between them it is a sorry lookout."

With these upbeat instructions did Warwickshire take the field at Old Trafford at noon on Thursday May 11th, 1911, to begin the Foster era. It started inauspiciously as the Bears limped to 91 for 6. The captain's contribution was typically extravagant. Batting at five, he strode suavely to the crease in ever-present silk cravat and to his first ball, from left-arm spinner James Heap (born in Burnley, died in Bolton), aimed a gargantuan mow and was bowled. A golden duck and a breathtaking statement of intent by the young captain.

Warwickshire totalled only 201 but then dismissed Lancashire for 155, a modest reply that owed much to another flash of glorious unpredictability from the skipper. Batting at three for Lancashire was the great Johnny Tyldesley, mainstay of England's batting and a legend of the Red Rose. He moved sweetly to 13 before Foster threw the ball to young batsman Jack Parsons. With no bowling record at all, Parsons was staggered to be asked to confront the maestro. Parsons to Tyldesley? Cannon fodder.

v. Northamptonshire at Northampton

Foster later recalled: "In his first over, Jack bowled the worst ball I have ever seen. What did Johnny do? He swung round his bat with his left hand - with his left hand only as much as to say 'this ball is no good' - and the ball went up in the air and Tiger Smith caught it." Foster's box of tricks was open.

To a first-innings lead of 46, Warwickshire added 369 second time around and bowled Lancashire out for 278 to win by 137 runs. The adventure was underway.

Foster's never-day-die spirit bore fruit in the third game, against Leicestershire at Edgbaston. By the final morning, the visitors were in command, 197 for 1 in their second innings, 145 runs ahead. But Foster and giant fast bowler Frank Field blasted out the last six wickets for 27 runs and Warwickshire reached their target of 266 for just one wicket. A stunning turnaround.

Next came Sussex at Coventry and another win rooted in tenacious refusal to accept defeat. Chasing 207 on a wet wicket, the Bears began the final day on 144 for 7. Foster was still there though and his skilful unbeaten 35 saw his side home by two wickets.

It was a remarkable start to his hegemony but the suspicion around the country that it would not last was highlighted by the next two matches; defeats to Worcestershire (by 116 runs at New Road) and Yorkshire (by four wickets at Edgbaston). Warwickshire hit back with a 14-run win over Derbyshire at Blackwell but a three-wicket defeat to Gloucestershire at Gloucester left their record at won four, lost four. Kent, champions for the previous two years, were clear at the top. But Foster's Warwickshire team was swept into the cricket pantheon by a sensational roll from late June.

The charge began on June 29th when Hampshire visited Edgbaston. Septimus Kinneir's unbeaten 268 lifted Warwickshire to 554 for 7 and Kinneir's tally alone would have beaten Hampshire by an innings as they crumbled all out for 132 and 126. Field rounded off the rout in spectacular fashion as three fast, straight 'uns ousted tail-enders Dudley Evans, John Newman and Eric Olivier for a hat-trick.

After a home draw with Surrey, Northamptonshire were brushed aside at Edgbaston with Foster and Field sharing match

173

figures of 59.3-14-171-16. At Chichester, Kinneir hit a century in each innings (the first Warwickshire player to do so) to set up an 81-run triumph over Sussex. Twelve thousand spectators were inside Edgbaston for the opening day of the next game, against Gloucestershire. Three days later another win was safely bagged thanks to Foster's input of 22.2-5-76-5, 25-8-59-3 and 56 and 87. Mighty Yorkshire were swept aside by 198 runs at Harrogate (Field 7 for 20) before draws with Hampshire and Worcestershire brought a slight check to the momentum. Warwickshire approached their last four games - against Derbyshire, Lancashire, Leicestershire and Northamptonshire - almost certainly needing to win them all. Four thumping victories - three by an innings - did the trick.

The home match against Derbyshire required another mighty fightback. It all seemed to have gone pear-shaped by the close of the first day when Derbyshire were 166 for 2, having rattled the Bears out for 170. Two days later Warwickshire were celebrating a 165-run victory, which shone even brighter when news arrived from Canterbury that Kent had lost to Lancashire. If Warwickshire won their last three matches, they would be champs.

Lancashire left their good form in the Garden of England and were demolished by Field's 12 wickets in an innings-and-40-run success. Only a day and a half was required to dispose of Leicestershire by an innings and 54 runs at Hinckley. So Warwickshire reached Northampton knowing that victory would secure the title.

Foster won the toss and controversially (95 per cent of captains chose to bat in those days) inserted Northamptonshire. He promptly knocked out William Denton's middle stump with the first ball of the match. Two hours later Foster had 5 for 18 and Field 4 for 27 and Northamptonshire were all out for 73. By the close Warwickshire were 226 for 6 with Crowther Charlesworth batting like a king and the championship all but won.

But wait. Monday's play was lost to rain. Could it be that they were to be thwarted in the cruellest fashion of all? On Monday night Foster and his team, too tense to sleep, stayed up drinking and playing cards right through to dawn. Then they attacked breakfast in the highest of spirits having watched Tuesday arrive bright and sunny. Cricket there would certainly be - and they made short work of finishing the job. After Charlesworth extended his innings to 130 the F-force got busy. Foster took 6 for 63 and Field 3 for 60, Warwickshire were the champions and cavorting about this very Northampton turf just like Knight, Brown, Trott and Co did today. Magnificent stuff.

And compared to it, what happened here between 10.30a.m. and six o'clockish on September 16th, 2004, was on the invisible side of anonymous. With the trophy presentation looming post-play, the cricket resembled some strange preparatory ritual conducted by rote before an audience comprised mostly of Warwickshire supporters interspersed with a few diehard, parka-clad home members.

Warwickshire won their 13th toss out of 16 (what a contrast to the 1972 champo-winning Bears who won only four out of 20) and batted. Knight dropped down the order to allow Ian Westwood, on his championship debut, to open and the 22-year-old's first championship runs were soon punched through the covers off the back-foot off Johann Louw. The South African's revenge soon arrived. Westwood nicked his 13th delivery to trigger a collapse to 69 for 5. Perhaps the celebrations had preceded the presentation.

Powell, Troughton, Brown and Frost organised a revival. Brown alone built his innings beyond 50 and the Scot was closing in on a century and 1,000 runs for the season (he started this match needing another 151) as he reached stumps unbeaten on 95 with 19 fours. Seam bowler Nick Warren, meanwhile, like Westwood making his championship debut, experienced a quiet first day on the circuit. He warmed up, ate lunch and watched.

Friday, September 17th: No play.

Last night's celebrations were, of course, conducted in the best possible taste and with a degree of restraint appropriate to finely honed, ultra-professional sportsmen. Warwickshire's players were all there razor-sharp and fresh as daisies ready for play at 10.30a.m. on the dot but to their enormous disappointment, it was raining.

The Year of the Bear

Rain in Northampton. How spooky is that? When the Bears clinched the champo here in 1911 the second day was washed out - and now the second day is washed out again. Makes you think.

Now throw in these facts. It was a victory over Northamptonshire, allied to defeat for nearest challengers Yorkshire against Worcestershire at Scarborough, that clinched the title for Tom Dollery's side in 1951. And a key plank of the 1994 success under Dermot Reeve was a titanic four-wicket win at Northampton (Brian Lara struck a run-a-ball 197, Tim Munton took 10 wickets in the match then, thanks largely to Dominic Ostler, the Bears reached a target of 228 in 38 overs with three balls to spare). Maybe Warwickshire's hopes of retaining the title in 2005 will be damaged by the absence of fixtures against their neighbours to the south-east, who will be in Division Two.

At least today's washout has virtually ensured that the Bears will remain unbeaten through a whole championship season for the first time since 1972. And it ensured that everyone was nice and fresh for the traditional end-of-season team pizz-up and fines night tonight.

Saturday, September 18th:

Warwickshire 295. Northamptonshire 233 for 7.

Brown soon acquired the five runs he needed to complete his century but ran out of partners (on 108 from 172 balls with 22 fours) still 43 short of 1,000 first-class runs for the season. Louw bowled Streak and Warren as the Bears recorded their lowest completed innings total of the season. They'll get over it.

Warren's maiden champo knock lasted two deliveries, but he made a bigger impression with the ball. This time last year Warwickshire invited the young seamer to find another county despite having another year left on his contract at Edgbaston. He chose to stay and fight for another deal, not easy with the Sword of Damocles poised above him and injury troubles affecting him. But buoyed by the faith, time and expertise of Steve Perryman, Warren reacted in exactly the right way, toughed it out and has got himself a new deal. His first spell today yielded a prosaic 7-2-

39-0, but his potential was evident from his second in a burst of three wickets for one run in 10 balls. Pitching the ball up and wobbling it around he bowled Brophy, trapped White lbw and found Phillips' outside-edge.

Brown had removed Northamptonshire's openers before Jeff Cook suffered the seldom-suffered fate of perishing to Trott, and Usman Afzaal edged Wagh. Sales kept an end up while Warren executed his flurry of damage and the captain will resume tomorrow morning on 48, but it was all rather flat. The long season has taken its toll. Much of Warwickshire's squad is affected by a bug and feeling under the weather. Westwood took a blow on the knee and Troughton slipped on the outfield, hurting his groin so Tahir and Carter (the latter just back from nipping round the corner to watch Northampton Saints play rugby) were called upon to field. Then Wagh damaged a finger so fitness coach Simon Hollyhead did a stint, reprising his previous outing as twelfth man at the Rose Bowl in 2002, a brilliant cameo that peaked with a panther-like pounce at mid-on to prevent Neil Johnson and John Crawley taking a single. Again today he gave an immaculate exhibition of the fielding art, something at least for Northamptonshire's shivering, suffering supporters to take away from a plain day.

Sunday, September 19th:

Northamptonshire 265. Warwickshire 109 for 5.

MATCH DRAWN:
NORTHAMPTONSHIRE 9 POINTS,
WARWICKSHIRE 9.

After the stupendous final day of the 1911 season Warwickshire's players travelled back to Birmingham by train full of elation and euphoria, to be greeted by huge crowds cheering and clapping and flinging their caps in the air. The generation of 2004 slipped quietly into their Peugeots and drove quietly back up the M1 to an oblivious city after a final day of the sort of eccentric Horsham-type futility that only cricket, among professional sport, can supply.

The Year of the Bear

The world's population (roughly 6,301,000,001 but it's difficult to count them because they keep moving around) appeared to have sussed what might happen because of that number, only a couple of hundred pointed their toes in the direction of Wantage Road. These were true enthusiasts though, while the esteemed members of Section 19 took the opportunity to toast this fine season one last time, one did wonder at the motives of some of the others present. Solitary figures, overcoated to the autumn chill, silently observing the death throes of a spent season. How will they fill the long, cold, empty winter days?

Even now in this draughty annexe of the summer the indefatigable Brown managed to come up with a story. He took the last two wickets this morning to finish with 5 for 53 - his second five-wicket haul of the season and only Warwickshire's fourth (including three against Northamptonshire). Just when everyone else was clocking off, Brown goes and records a 'five-for' and a century in the match.

After the home side had finished plodding drearily to 265, Warwickshire managed to outdo them in terms of dreary ploddingfulness. Or should that be ploddy drearitude? Anyway, whatever it was the Bears mastered it as Westwood decided to get some time in at the crease. His 38, occupying 147 balls in 157 minutes, offered pleasure only to his nearest and dearest. Brown, elevated in the order in pursuit of the 43 he needed for 1,000, edged his second ball to second slip. Bell also concluded his wonderful season with a second-ball dismissal.

Trott then took root. God, how he took root. He faced 116 balls, only one of which reached the boundary. Incredibly, as the score crawled past 100 in the 60th over, there were still some spectators present. David Sales had a bowl. Usman Afzaal had a bowl. Tim Roberts had a bowl. When wicket-keeper Gerard Brophy removed his gauntlets to deliver his first over in first-class cricket it really was time to pack up.

****

v. Northamptonshire at Northampton

SCORECARD

Warwickshire 1st innings

MA Wagh	c Brophy	b Louw	7
IJ Westwood	c Brophy	b Louw	3
IR Bell	c Cook	b Rofe	24
IJL Trott		b Brown	15
*NV Knight		b Louw	20
MJ Powell	lbw	b Cook	49
JO Troughton	c Sales	b Brown	27
DR Brown	not out		108
+T Frost		b Phillips	23
HH Streak		b Louw	14
NA Warren		b Louw	0
Extras	(b 3, nb 2)		5
		Total	**295**
			all out

FoW: 1-5, 2-18, 3-43, 4-69, 5-69, 6-115, 7-197, 8-246, 9-295, 10-295.

Louw 20.4-2-93-5, Rofe 28-9-63-1, Phillips 19-11-36-1, Brown 35-11-67-2, Cook 7-1-23-1, White 3-0-10-0.

Northamptonshire 1st innings

TW Roberts	c Wagh	b Brown	46
TB Huggins		b Brown	34
JW Cook	lbw	b Trott	51
U Afzaal	c Frost	b Wagh	19
*DJG Sales	not out		72
+GL Brophy		b Warren	23
AR White	lbw	b Warren	0
BJ Phillips	c Frost	b Warren	0
J Louw	c Frost	b Brown	5
PC Rofe	c Bell	b Brown	4
JF Brown	lbw	b Brown	0
Extras	(lb 6, w 1, nb 4)		11
		Total	**265**
			all out

FoW: 1-79, 2-84, 3-129, 4-189, 5-230, 6-230, 7-232, 8-255, 9-265, 10-265.

Streak 17-2-62-0, Brown 20.3-3-53-5, Warren 17-3-60-3, Bell 5-2-17-0, Wagh 10-2-37-1, Troughton 3-0-10-0, Trott 8-1-20-0.

Warwickshire 2nd innings

MA Wagh		b Phillips	19
IJ Westwood	c Louw	b White	38
DR Brown	c Afzaal	b Phillips	0
IR Bell	lbw	b Brown	1
IJL Trott	not out		38
*NV Knight		b White	3
MJ Powell	not out		5
Extras	(lb 3, nb 2		5
		Total	**109**
			for 5

JO Troughton, HH Streak, +T Frost and NA Warren did not bat.

FoW: 1-36, 2-36, 3-37, 4-87, 5-96.

Louw 7-2-18-0, Rofe 3-2-2-0, Brown 26-8-47-1, Phillips 8-3-10-2, White 15-3-19-2, Sales 2-1-2-0, Afzaal 2.3-1-7-0, Roberts 1-1-0-0, Roberts 1-0-1-0.

Umpires: DJ Constant and B Leadbeater.

****

AVERAGES 2004

Batting and Fielding

Name	Ms	I	NO	Runs	HS	Ave	SR	100	50	Ct	St
IR Bell	15	25	4	1498	262*	71.33	57.70	6	4	6	-
AF Giles	1	1	0	70	70	70.00	55.55	-	1	-	-
GB Hogg	11	12	2	662	158	66.20	96.92	1	7	4	-
NV Knight	15	28	6	1256	303*	57.09	56.29	2	8	9	-
IJL Trott	16	27	6	1126	115	53.61	53.84	1	10	11	-
DR Brown	16	21	3	911	62	50.61	55.48	3	2	7	-
MJ Powell	9	15	2	630	134	48.46	40.28	2	2	4	-
T Frost	16	18	5	488	135*	37.53	53.15	1	1	44	4
MA Wagh	16	29	2	928	167	34.37	57.03	1	5	14	-
JO Troughton	13	16	0	528	120	33.00	47.48	1	4	2	-
HH Streak	6	9	2	180	61	25.71	41.09	-	1	-	-
NM Carter	13	15	4	245	95	22.27	93.15	-	1	3	-
N Tahir	11	12	5	150	49	21.42	31.38	-	-	1	-
IJ Westwood	1	2	0	41	38	20.50	25.62	-	-	-	-
A Richardson	7	4	2	26	17	13.00	30.95	-	-	2	-
D Pretorius	9	6	3	31	14	10.33	38.75	-	-	1	-
NA Warren	1	1	0	0	0	0.00	0.00	-	-	-	-

Bowling

Name	Ms	O	M	R	W	Ave	Best	5	10	SR	Econ
NA Warren	1	17	3	60	3	20.00	3-60	-	-	34.30	3.52
HH Streak	6	159	29	522	24	21.75	7-80	2	1	39.7	3.28
IR Bell	15	137.4	32	400	14	28.57	4-4	-	-	59.0	2.90
IJL Trott	16	23	5	86	3	28.66	1-1	-	-	46.0	3.73
N Tahir	11	194.4	26	766	26	29.46	4-43	-	-	44.9	3.93
AF Giles	1	62	17	128	4	32.00	3-55	-	-	93.0	2.06
DR Brown	16	412.4	91	1273	38	33.50	5-53	2	-	65.1	3.08
D Pretorius	9	245	43	936	24	39.00	4-119	-	-	61.2	3.82
NM Carter	13	349.4	71	1189	27	44.03	4-50	-	-	77.7	3.40
MA Wagh	16	281.4	44	977	18	54.27	3-85	-	-	93.8	3.46
GB Hogg	11	256.2	39	881	14	62.92	4-90	-	-	109.8	3.43
A Richardson	7	144	28	532	6	88.66	2-62	-	-	144.0	3.69
JO Troughton	13	123	27	344	3	114.66	2-106	-	-	246.0	2.79
MJ Powell	9	8	0	51	0	-	-	-	-	-	6.37

Frizzell County Championship
Division One

	P	W	L	D	Bat	Bowl	Ded	Pts
Warwicks	16	5	0	11	65	43	0.0	222.0
Kent	16	7	3	6	43	41	0.0	206.0
Surrey	16	5	5	6	60	42	0.5	195.5
Middlesex	16	4	4	8	48	43	0.0	179.0
Sussex	16	4	5	7	46	42	0.0	172.0
Gloucs	16	3	3	10	49	41	0.0	172.0
Worcesters	16	3	6	7	51	40	0.0	161.0
Lancashire	16	2	4	10	44	44	2.0	154.0
Northampton	16	1	4	11	35	41	0.0	134.0

HOW THEY PERFORMED

SEPTEMBER 2004

NEIL ABBERLEY.
There can be fewer better tributes to a batting coach than the lorry-load of batting records that Warwickshire shattered in 2004.

IAN BELL.
After a slow start went on to record just about the perfect season. Passed 100 six times in the course of his 1,498 championship runs - at an average of 71.33 - to earn a Test match debut in which he shone. Helped his beloved Bears to the title and graduated fully into the England set-up. Warwickshire might not see too much of "Belly" for the next decade.

DOUGIE BROWN.
Massive input to the triumph in many ways, as pointed out by coach John Inverarity in the foreword to this book. Leading wicket-taker with 38, bowled most overs, and averaged 50.61 with the bat. One of four ever-presents and a real driving force.

NEIL CARTER.
Twenty-seven championship wickets at 44.03 are not world-beating figures, but Carter delivered some vital spells, notably in the victories at home to Surrey and against Middlesex at Lord's, that really got the title momentum going.

TONY FROST.
Ever-present, comfortably kept Keith Piper at bay by lodging a batting average of 37.53 and snaring 48 victims with the gloves. Dug deep under huge pressure in the home game with Sussex to bat out for the draw, which virtually killed-off the Bears' last challenger.

ASHLEY GILES.
Squeezed in one championship match, at home to Surrey, among his glorious summer exploits for England. His 70 runs and four wickets contributed plenty to building the sensational victory that set the season in motion.

BRAD HOGG.
Batted wonderfully from the first ball he faced. Fielded with energy and always eager behind the scenes to help younger players with their game. Bowling? Er, room for improvement.

SIMON HOLLYHEAD.
The championship quest was helped immeasurably by injuries touching the senior players only very lightly. That was down to Hollyhead and Gerhard Mostert.

JOHN INVERARITY.
Massively respected by the players - that's why he got the best out of them. Deep and astute thinker about cricket, his quiet exterior masks a mentality of considerable steel. Forged immediate and fruitful alliance with the captain.

NICK KNIGHT.
Dream start to the captaincy. Underpinned the triumph with a flood of runs in May and June and cajoled his side into keeping going until they were over the finishing line, despite some tiring limbs and fading form.

GERHARD MOSTERT.
The fitness regimes worked so well that he enjoyed his quietest season at Warwickshire so far.

STEVE PERRYMAN.
In a batsmen-dominated season the bowling coach strived hard to get the best out of limited resources. Provided wise counsel to Inverarity and Knight.

MICHAEL POWELL.
Had a major stake in the success, not just for his input with the bat when his chances arrived, but for all the groundwork laid towards the 2004 triumph in the three preceding years when Powell was captain.

DEWALD PRETORIUS.
Did not knock over enough top-order batsmen with the first new ball, but delivered some big-hearted spells. Showed enough to suggest he can improve upon figures of 24 wickets at 39 each with a strike-rate of 61.25.

ALAN RICHARDSON.
Poignantly, in a great season for the county, a player who has never given less than 100 per cent ended with an invitation to look for another employer. Richardson's rhythm was never quite right in 2004, and Naqaash Tahir's emergence shunted him out of the first-team. Joined Middlesex in November.

HEATH STREAK.
Arrived on the back of an intensely difficult time in Zimbabwe and was then frustrated by a stomach-muscle injury after his spectacular debut against Northamptonshire. Rapidly endeared himself to his new teammates with consummate professionalism.

NAQAASH TAHIR.
The find of the season. A wicket-taking bowler and a batsman of sound technique and temperament. Quiet member of the dressing room, but made a big impression on the field.

JONATHAN TROTT.
Knight and Bell scored the big runs but Trott was scarcely less important to the batting unit. Started strongly when others were still chipping-off the rust and was still scoring important runs in the key games late on.

JIM TROUGHTON.
A testing year. Lost his place in June, albeit unluckily as he had scored half-centuries in three of the previous four championship games, but seized his chance when it came again with a vital century at Bristol.

MARK WAGH.
Mixed season. A midsummer purple patch earned him selection in England's provisional 30-strong squad for the ICC Trophy, but a poor run-in saw him fail to seize the moment.

DAVID WAINWRIGHT.
Scored with his customary panache, resilience and accuracy whether operating in Test venue splendour, caravan or tent.

MILESTONES FROM THE 2004 SEASON

Compiled by Robert Brooke

Warwickshire's average runs per wicket in 2004 - 47.74 - was their highest ever in the championship, surpassing the previous best of 42.10 in 1994. Only twice have they ever exceeded 40 runs per wicket in a season.

It was also the highest average runs per wicket by any county champions, surpassing the 44.90 achieved by Lancashire in 1928. Strangely, in 2004 Warwickshire's bowlers also posted the highest average runs per wicket taken - 40.06, comfortably surpassing the previous highest of 34.26 by Middlesex in 1990.

Warwickshire's run of ten scores of 400-plus in consecutive matches, starting with the home game against Surrey, is a record for any team in county cricket.

The aggregate runs in the home game with Worcestershire - 1,286 - was the highest ever without an individual century in a Warwickshire game, surpassing the previous record of 1,225 against Nottinghamshire at Trent Bridge in 2003.

When Warwickshire beat Surrey by seven wickets at Edgbaston it was only the second time they have beaten a team that had scored totals in excess of 300 and 400.

When three players - Ian Bell, Michael Powell and Dougie Brown - hit centuries in the same innings, against Surrey at

The Year of the Bear

Guildford, it equalled the Bears' record, along with 16 other instances, for century-makers in an innings.

Nick Knight's unbeaten 303 against Middlesex at Lord's was a record for a Warwickshire number one in first-class cricket, surpassing Michael Powell's 236 against Oxford University at The Parks in 2001. At ten hours 44 minutes it was also the longest innings ever played for Warwickshire, nine minutes longer than the previous record, Mark Wagh's 315 also against Middlesex at Lord's three years earlier.

Tony Frost's unbeaten 135 against Sussex at Horsham was the best by a Warwickshire number eight, surpassing the 128 not out of Ashley Giles against Sussex at Hove in 2000.

During the season Ian Bell became the 14th Warwickshire batsman to score a century in each innings of a match, the eighth to score centuries in three successive innings and the fifth to score four centuries in five innings. He also became the youngest Warwickshire player to score a double-century, when he hit 262 not out against Sussex at Horsham at the age of 22 years and 29 days. He broke the 93-year-old record of Frank Foster, who was 22 years and 153 days old when he hit 200 against Surrey at Edgbaston in 1911. Bell was also the youngest player to score a century for the Bears.

Bell and Knight became the third and fourth players, behind Fred Gardner and Dougie Brown, to pass 50 in six successive innings.

Bell and Trott scored 1,000 runs in a season for the first time.

Warwickshire built 31 century stands during the season, eclipsing the previous record of 26 set in 1990. Bell was involved in 11, Trott 9, Knight and Wagh 8, Powell 6, Brown and Hogg 5, Troughton 4, Frost 3 and Streak, Tahir and Giles one each.

Three players posted career-best innings: Knight 303 not out, Bell 262 not out and Frost 135 not out. Two posted career-best bowling figures: Bell 4 for 4 against Middlesex at Lord's and Nick Warren 3 for 60 against Northamptonshire at Northampton.

Heath Streak's match bowling analysis of 13 for 158 is the best by any bowler on his debut for a county in championship cricket, surpassing the 12 for 92 by Archibald Fargus for Gloucestershire against Middlesex at Lord's in 1900.

Bibliography

100 Greats of Warwickshire CCC
(Robert Brooke),
Birmingham Post and Mail,
Lord's 1787-1945
(Sir Pelham Warner),
Cricketarchive.com,
The History of Warwickshire County Cricket Club
(Jack Bannister),
Twenty-Four Years of Cricket
(Arthur A.Lilley),
WG Grace
(Eric Midwinter),
Wisden Cricketers' Almanack,
Wisden Book of Obituaries